WHEN THE ENEMY STRIKES

WORKBOOK

THE KEYS TO WINNING YOUR SPIRITUAL BATTLES

CHARLES STANLEY

NELSON IMPACT
A Division of Thomas Nelson Publishers
Since 1798

www.thomasnelson.com

Published by Nelson Impact, a Division of Thomas Nelson, Inc., P.O. Box 141000, Nashville, Tennessee, 37214.

ISBN: 1-4185-0589-7

Printed in the United States of America.

05 06 07 08 09 — 9 8 7 6 5 4 3 2 1

CONTENTS

—⟿—

INTRODUCTION

—◈—

Remember the story of the artist who won a contest for the best picture of "peace"? Unlike the other entrants, who produced images of family picnics and brilliant sunsets, he painted a raging storm battering a barren cliff beside the sea. On a small recess in the rock he put a single flower, shielded by an overhang, raising a tiny blossom in utter disregard for the wind and rain.

Recently I heard of a lady who gave the people in her Bible study group a similar challenge, except that they were to draw their version of "evil." One older gentleman, normally a ready participant, seemed to be doing very little with his pencil and eventually handed the lady a blank sheet of paper, with a small frame around the edge. She held his entry until last, but soon she had commented on all the other images of monsters, Hitler look-alikes, and venomous snakes.

"Why, James?" she asked at last. "Why a blank page?"

"Because I think that the worst evil of all is the evil we cannot see," he said. "It blends in so well with other things it can fool us even when we're the most careful."

That fellow knew exactly what he was talking about. Let us search together for ways to recognize the face of evil in all its near-invisible forms.

Better still, let's examine the ways God has provided for us to protect ourselves. Let's build our awareness, our defenses, and our dependence on God Himself.

1

—⚬—

THE FACE OF EVIL

Satan sometimes confronts us with 100 percent evil. The soldiers who liberated Hitler's concentration camps at the end of World War II knew they were looking into the face of evil when they saw what had happened there.

In more recent years, no one who knows of the murderous actions of Idi Amin, Saddam Hussein, or the anti-Christian forces in Sudan, Rwanda, and other troubled spots around the globe can doubt that 100 percent evil is just as alive and active today as it was in biblical times.

Just as surely, on September 11, 2001, all those who watched those three airplanes crashing into the World Trade Center, the Pentagon, and that barren field in Pennsylvania knew they were seeing purest evil in action.

Or did they?

With respect to 9-11, many people actually blamed the United States for causing its own tragedy. "We are too proud and arrogant," they said. "We failed to be understanding and tolerant enough."

DOES EVIL COME IN DIFFERENT SIZES AND SHAPES?

Is evil, as in the adage about beauty, really "in the eyes of the beholder"? Or does it have a face, a name, and common methods of operation?

Let's study several examples of evil from the Bible, beginning with Genesis 4:23, 24. Please fill in the blanks.

Then Lamech said to his wives: "Adah and Zillah, hear my voice; Wives of Lamech, listen to my speech! For I have _____ a man for _____ me, Even a young man for _____ me. If Cain shall be avenged sevenfold, Then Lamech seventy-sevenfold" (NKJV).

(1) When Lamech said "If Cain shall be avenged sevenfold," to what "avenger" was he referring?

_____

_____

_____

(2) How did Lamech sin in both his actions and his words?

_____

_____

_____

(3) Can you identify anything in Lamech's story that indicates any cause of the sin other than the presence of pure evil?

_____

_____

_____

STRAIGHT FROM THE BOOK . . .

If you have made a commitment to Jesus as your Savior and Lord, you are absolutely correct in saying that your spirit already belongs to God and the devil can lay no claim on your eternal destiny. The satanic forces can do other things to you, however.

Now turn to 1 Kings 3:23–27. This familiar story is about Solomon and the two women who claimed the same child as their son. Begin with Solomon's judgment and observe what the two women said in response.

And the king said, "The one says, 'This is my son, who lives, and your son is the dead one'; and the other says, 'No! But your son is the _____ one, and my son is the _____ one.'" Then the king said, "Bring me a sword." So they brought a sword before the king. And the king said, "Divide the _____ child in two, and give half to one, and half to the other." Then the woman whose son was _____ spoke to the king, for she yearned with compassion for her son; and she said, "O my lord, give her the living child, and by no means kill him!" But the other said, "Let him be neither mine nor yours, but divide him." So the king answered and said, "Give the first woman the living child, and by no means kill him; she is _____ _____ " (NKJV).

(1) This story is often quoted to prove Solomon's wisdom. What characteristics of evil does it also expose?

_____

_____

_____

(2) Why do you think evil so often believes it will not be revealed?

_____

_____

_____

≪≫Next, turn to Genesis 39:11–15 and consider the story of Joseph and Potiphar's wife.

But it happened about this time, when Joseph went into the house to do his work, and none of the men of the house was inside, that she caught him by _____ _____ , saying, "Lie with me." But he left his _____ in her hand, and fled and ran outside. And so it was, when she saw that he had left his _____ in her hand and fled outside, that she called to the men of her house and spoke to them, saying, "See, he has brought in to us a Hebrew to mock us. He came in to me to lie with me, and I cried out with a loud voice. And it happened, when he heard that I lifted my voice and cried out, that he left his garment with me, and fled and went outside" (NKJV).

(1) Is there anything in this story itself, or the surrounding verses in Genesis 39, that indicate that Potiphar's wife was obviously an evil person?

_____

_____

_____

(2) Was Joseph the victim of his own foolishness, or was something else at work here?

_____

_____

_____

(3) From what you might already know about the story of Joseph, what do you think about the devil's ability to kill Joseph immediately or to have him put into prison until he died?

_____

_____

_____

_____

✍ ONLY IN LIVING COLOR! ✍

One of our difficulties in discerning evil is that so much of what we encounter seems to come—not in black-and-white—but in shades of gray. Satan can be very adept at masking his temptations and covering up his intent.

In contrast, most of us think of evil in the Bible as easy-to-spot. There is some truth in that assumption, for much of the Bible deals in what we often call *universal types* or *clear examples* of evil—for teaching purposes.

Read the Scriptures listed in the following table, but don't be satisfied with the barest minimum of verses—read them in context, meaning that you might need to read several more verses to understand completely the whole story. For each one, try to give a one-word name to the evil it illustrates. Then rate that evil with a numerical *Visibility Index*, based on how easily you think it can be discerned. If it is clearly a black-and-white case, give it a 10. If it seems to be 90 percent evil, give it a 9. If it is half-and-half, give it a 5; and so on.

Keep in mind, however, that in spite of what Satan wants us to think, giving in to something that *seems* only 10 percent evil can be just as devastating, in the end, as giving in to something that is most obviously his work. Sometimes the visibility for Satan's handiwork is cloudy for us.

The first entry is filled out for you as an example.

Scripture	Name of Evil	What Happened?	Visibility Index
Gen. 4:8	Murder	Cain killed Abel	10
2 Sam. 11:6–13			
John 4:6–19			
Gen. 29—31			
Ex. 2:12			▼

▼

Num. 16:1–35	
Ex. 32:3, 4; 21–24	
1 Chr. 21:1, 17	
1 Sam. 20:5, 6	
2 Chr. 24:20–22	

⫘Next, consider the death of John the Baptist in Matthew 14:6–9.

But when _____ birthday was celebrated, the daughter of _____ danced before them and pleased Herod. Therefore he promised with an oath to give her whatever she might ask. So she, having been prompted by _____ _____, said, "Give me John the Baptist's head here on a platter." And the king was sorry; nevertheless, because of the oaths and because of those who sat with him, he commanded it to be given to her (NKJV).

(1) Evil does not always act alone. Three different people were involved in this case: _____, _____, and _____. Who was most responsible?

_____

_____

_____

(2) Who was *least* responsible?

_____

_____

_____

(3) Why?

_____

To change the outcome what small thing could each one have done differently?

_____

_____

_____

_____

_____

_____

(4) Now let's expand on this information by reviewing the beginning of Matthew 14. What was the evil that started the whole sequence leading to the death of John the Baptist?

_____

_____

_____

_____

> **STRAIGHT FROM THE BOOK . . .**
>
> *Behind every evil person and every evil act lurks the real enemy of your life. He exists in the spirit realm, and he is relentless in his pursuit of you. He is 100 percent evil, and he has a plan to destroy your life.*

(5) Was it an obvious or a hidden expression of evil?

_____

_____

_____

(6) What did John the Baptist try to do about it? Was he right or wrong to do so?

_____

_____

_____

_____

Another familiar story is found in Acts 5:1–5.

But a certain man named Ananias, with Sapphira his wife, sold a possession. And he kept back part of _____ _____, his wife also being aware of it, and brought a certain part and laid it at the apostles' feet. But Peter said, "Ananias, why has Satan filled your heart to lie to the Holy Spirit and keep back part of the price of the land for _____? While it remained, was it not your own? And after it was sold, was it not in your own control? Why have you conceived this thing in your heart? You have not lied to men but to God." Then Ananias, hearing these words, fell down and breathed his last (NKJV).

Clearly, a lie is an evil thing. Yet in all the years that have passed since this first-century event, millions of people have lied but not paid any great price—at least, not in their earthly lives. Many people have tried to understand why Ananias and Sapphira were punished by God so severely and so quickly.

Keeping in mind the context of the *entire* story, why do you think it happened the way it did?

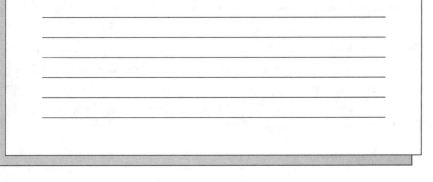

DO WE ALL HAVE A CONSCIENCE?

Jeremiah 31:33 says: "But this is the covenant that I will make with the house of Israel after those days, says the LORD: I will put My law in their minds, and write it on their hearts; and I will be their God, and they shall be My people (NKJV).

Most people agree that this verse refers to what we now call conscience. They believe that by "writing His law on our hearts" God gave to each of us an inbuilt awareness of right and wrong. Certainly this seems to be true—most people do not need to be told, for example, that murder is simply wrong.

Or do they? Given the tragedy of 9-11, the vicious bombings of innocent Israelis and the random killings that seem to be going on somewhere in the world at almost any time, does this mean that God no longer writes "His law" on the hearts of men and women? Write what you think in the space below.

_____

_____

_____

_____

_____

_____

YOUR ENEMY HAS A NAME AND A PURPOSE

The evil that we have examined so far comes in many forms and acts in many ways. Whether evil works through one person alone (Lamech) or through a small group of people (Herod, Herodias, and her daughter), all evil derives from one source only: the evil spirit we call Satan.

The name *Satan* comes from the title he was given in the ancient Hebrew language: *Ha Satan*, meaning the *adversary*. As long as we refuse to serve him, Satan will be our adversary in every aspect of our lives and in everything we say and do. In fact, even those who do serve him can never be sure that he will live up to any promises he makes.

⋙ A BEING OF 100 PERCENT EVIL ⋘

Actually, there is much evidence to suggest that Satan remains our adversary whether or not we serve him. Remember, he is a being of 100 percent evil, driven by nothing but his own perverted desires for power, respect, and revenge. There is no honor, no sense of fairness, no compassion for others, no respect for anyone else's viewpoint, no caring about anyone else's needs—in short, no good whatsoever in any portion or part of him.

If we could build the longest teeter-totter (Look that word up if you're not familiar with it!) in the universe, extending to the farthest reaches of our own solar system (which, of course, encompasses only a small portion of what God has created), Satan would be at one end, and God would be at the other. Satan's end of the board, of course, would be high in the air, and he would be jumping up and down, screaming and demanding that all the rest of us climb on his end to give him more leverage.

However, even if we all joined him, he would never be able to dislodge God and gain control.

FOR DEEPER CONSIDERATION . . .

If you are in a group setting, talk about some of the evils most prevalent in your city or locality. Name them, discuss how Satan tries to hide their true nature, and consider how best to avoid being taken in by them.

In the first place, he has only as much power as he can steal from us. In comparison to God Himself, Satan is truly a weakling. In the second place, his evil nature is so absolute that if he did have unlimited power, he would not use it for good—certainly not for yours or for mine.

The reason is even more basic. Satan has only one purpose: to defy, outsmart, and literally to *replace* the true God of the universe in every way he can at every hour of every day. Satan does not sleep or rest; neither does he miss opportunities to oppose God. As God is love, Satan is hatred. As God is just, Satan is unjust. As God is always the same, Satan changes his outer facade constantly, coming and going in a thousand disguises and a thousand deceptive voices.

✍️Look up the following verses in the Bible and write the name for Satan that each one reveals:

❑ Genesis 3:1 _____

❑ Isaiah 14:4 _____

❑ Matthew 4:3 _____

❑ Matthew 13:19 _____

❑ Matthew 13:39 _____

❑ John 8:44 _____

❑ 2 Corinthians 4:4 _____

❑ Colossians 1:13 _____

❑ 1 Peter 5:8 _____

❑ Revelation 12:9 _____,

and _____

Only Christ Himself is referred to in Scripture by so many names. The difference, of course, is that all the names by which Christ is known are complimentary. They are terms of respect and affection. They speak of His glory, His power, His love. From the verses above we notice that the exact opposite is true of Satan.

(1) Of all the names for Satan in these verses, how many are positive?

_____

_____

_____

(2) Which of those names describe or suggest a negative aspect—something to be feared or avoided?

_____

_____

_____

_____

Unfortunately, Satan cannot always be avoided, but he *can* be defeated.

STRAIGHT FROM THE BOOK . . .

For years some people have talked about God in rather euphemistic terms. He's their Higher Power, the Force, or the Man Upstairs. The truth is, good has a name, and His name is God. Evil also has a name. His name is Satan or the devil. Satan literally refers to a "snitch" who accuses you, betrays you, and brings about your downfall. The devil refers to a spiritual being who is the supreme personification of evil.

WE CANNOT WIN ON OUR OWN!

The fight against evil is not physical, but spiritual (Eph. 6:12). We have no hope of winning spiritual battles without God. He can take any physical form He wishes: He and Satan are both spirit beings. However, one thing that elevates this whole equation from the *simple* to the *profound* is that God can turn Satan's efforts completely around and use them for good!

✎Read Genesis 50:19–21 again, but especially verse 20. Turn to that verse now and write it in the blanks below.

_____ _____ _____ _____ _____

_____ _____ _____ _____ _____

_____ _____ _____ _____ _____

_____ (Gen. 50:20, NKJV).

In just 31 words (in the *New King James Version*), most of them only one syllable in length, Joseph speaks to the same brothers who sold him into slavery many years earlier. In the simplest possible terms he explains how God turned the evil they embraced into something good.

Even those once-deceitful brothers, now repentant, were among those whose lives were saved by Joseph's "prior positioning" in the land of Egypt.

Truly, the Creator of the Universe is a far greater spiritual force than anything this world (and Satan is truly *of this world!*) can bring against us.

FOR DEEPER CONSIDERATION . . .

Genesis 3:22 says: "Then the LORD God said, "Behold, the man has become like one of Us, to know good and evil . . ." (NKJV).

In the modern era we teach our children the difference between good and evil because we believe it's necessary for them to know. But God clearly created man without this inbuilt knowledge—the sin of Adam and Eve introduced that knowledge as what modern merchandisers might call an "add-on."

What does that mean—did God intend to teach man about good and evil eventually, or was it His original desire for mankind to remain forever innocent? What would be the advantages and disadvantages of such a permanent "condition"? Could we ever be "as one with God" without such knowledge?

_____

_____

_____

_____

_____

_____

WORDS TO REMEMBER . . .

I do not pray that You should take them out of the world, but that You should keep them from the evil one. They are not of the world, just as I am not of the world. Sanctify them by Your truth. Your word is truth (John 17:15–17, NKJV).

CLOSING PRAYER . . .

—w—

Our Father, help us to recognize the differences between good and evil, especially in those times when our adversary works so hard to hide his evil intent from our sight. Keep us close beside You, and lend to our limited senses a greater portion of Your divine wisdom. Enhance our ability to see Satan, always, for what he truly is.

In Jesus' name, Amen.

2

THE NATURE OF OUR ENEMY

We live in an age that does not recognize absolutes. According to modern secular thinking, the highest principle we can pursue is "tolerance" of all viewpoints. This is especially true in anything having to do with God and the nature of good and evil.

However, moral absolutes are real. God is real. His Word is real, and the spiritual laws He laid out for all mankind thousands of years ago are as real now as they were when He gave them to Moses on Mt. Sinai. Let's look to God's Word to clarify this issue.

THE DEVIL IS REAL!

☜Turn to Job 1:6–12 and fill in the blanks below.

Now there was a day when the _____ _____ _____ came to present themselves before the LORD, and _____ also came among them. And the LORD said to Satan, "From where do you come?" So Satan answered the LORD and said, "From going _____ _____ _____ on the earth, and from walking back and forth on it." Then the LORD said to Satan, "Have you considered My servant Job, that there is none like him on the earth, a

_____ blameless and upright man, one who fears God and shuns evil?" So Satan answered the LORD and said, "Does Job fear God for nothing? Have You not made a _____ around him, around his household, and around all that he has on every side? You have blessed the work of his hands, and his _____ have increased in the land. But now, stretch out Your hand and touch all that he has, and he will surely curse You to Your face!" And the LORD said to Satan, "Behold, all that he has is _____ _____ _____; only do not lay a hand on his person."   So Satan went out from the _____ of the LORD (NKJV).

Can any biblical passage be clearer about the reality of Satan's existence?

Note that in verse 12 God specifically said to Satan that He would put all that Job had "in your [i.e., Satan's] power." From this we understand that Satan's power is much more limited in all other cases. Could this limitation be why he depends so much on deception?

THE DEVIL IS INVISIBLE

Satan has no physical form, but we can still encounter him in a number of ways. In addition to using other people to do his work, he himself can affect all aspects of our beings—body, soul, and spirit. Thus many of our physical misfortunes are brought about by his manipulations of our intellect, emotions, and will.

Satan is a spirit being. Many times he can also appear to be attacking us through our spirits, though he cannot attack our spirits directly.

One major reason is that God is a spirit being Himself! In fact, if you accept God's offer of salvation, Christ Himself sends the Holy Spirit to reside within your own spirit. Thus you might think of the invisible, spiritual part of your being as your own "direct pipeline" to God. The Holy Spirit's main purpose is to provide a constant source of help to you in all times of trouble, through that direct connection.

The passage from Job, which gives us the details of Satan's "bargain" with God, also tells us several things about the vast differences between them. The Bible makes the nature of God, as all-powerful Creator and "24/7 would-be Participant" in our lives, clear in many other places as well.

For example, in Colossians 1:15, 16 Paul says of Christ:

He is the image of the _____ God, the firstborn over all creation. For by Him all things were created that are in heaven and that are on earth, visible and invisible, whether _____ or _____ or _____ or _____. All things were created through Him and for Him (NKJV).

In Romans 1:20, Paul writes:

For since the creation of the world His _____ _____ are clearly seen, being understood by the things that are made, even His _____ power and Godhead, so that they [i.e., those who still refuse to honor God and accept His salvation] are without excuse, . . . (NKJV).

And Timothy 1:17 says:

Now to the King _____, _____, _____, to God who alone is wise, be honor and glory forever and ever. Amen (NKJV).

(1) What message about the nature and the power of God do all three of these scriptural passages (plus the first passage from Job) have in common?

_____

_____

_____

_____

(2) What comfort can we take from that same message?

_____

_____

_____

Your spirit is the aspect of yourself that never passes away, through which you were intended to commune directly with God, both here on Earth and throughout eternity.

The best Satan can do is to "clog the pipeline" with things that prevent us from worshiping God *in spirit and in truth*, as we are instructed to do in John 4:23 (NKJV). For this Satan is very well-organized! He also never quite gives up, no matter how well we are able to resist his enticements at any given moment.

> ### STRAIGHT FROM THE BOOK . . .
>
> *A satanic attack is a deliberate, willful, intentional, and well-designed act intended to bring harm to a person in any way—physical, mental, economic, relational, or spiritual.*

THE DEVIL IS ORGANIZED

Consider the opening verses of the fourth chapter of Luke, in Luke 4:1, 2.

Then Jesus, being filled with the Holy Spirit, returned from the Jordan and was led by the Spirit into the wilderness, being _____ for forty days by the devil. And in those days He ate nothing, and afterward, when they had ended, He was hungry (NKJV).

Notice how the devil waited quietly, not saying a word through all the above, until he felt Jesus was physically worn down and therefore spiritually vulnerable as well (or so the devil thought!). The story continues in Luke 4:3, 4.

And the devil said to Him, "If You are the Son of God, _____ this stone to become bread."

> But Jesus answered him, saying, "It is written, 'Man shall not __________ __________ __________ alone, but by every word of God'" (NKJV).

Again it seems that Satan has been checkmated, but as Luke 4:5–8 reveals, he does not give up.

> Then the devil, taking Him up on a high mountain, showed Him all the __________ of the world in a moment of time. And the devil said to Him, "All this __________ I will give You, and their glory; for this has been delivered to me, and I give it to whomever I wish. Therefore, if You will __________ before me, all will be Yours."
>
> And Jesus answered and said to him, "Get behind Me, Satan! For it is written, 'You shall worship the LORD your God, and Him only you shall serve'"(NKJV).

Finally, Satan plays his last card in Luke 4:9–13 . . .

> Then he brought Him to Jerusalem, set Him on the pinnacle of the __________, and said to Him, "If You are the Son of God, throw Yourself down from here. For it is written:
>
> 'He shall give His angels charge over you, to keep you,' and, 'In their hands they shall bear you up, lest you dash your foot against a stone.'"
>
> And Jesus answered and said to him, "It has been said, 'You shall not __________ the LORD your God.'" Now when the devil had ended every __________, he departed from Him until an opportune time (NKJV).

Among other things, this passage illustrates several important things about Satan. List three or four in the spaces below, and briefly explain your reasoning.

____

_____

_____

_____

If you concluded at least two or three things, (1) that the devil uses definite plans of attack and (2) that he never gives up, and (3) that Satan has *his* version of Scripture, you are correct. Now, based on your own personal experience, can you think of a time when Satan pursued you relentlessly over the course of many weeks or months? Did he finally prevail, even if only for a moment? Write about your experience in the space below:

THE DEVIL IS CRAFTY AND SCHEMING

The Old Testament story of David shows how hard Satan was willing to work to seduce him and ruin God's plan to bring Christ Himself, the Savior of all mankind, from the lineage of David. The full story is fascinating and instructive. Every once in a while I like to refresh my memory by rereading it, and I recommend the same to you. You can begin with the 17th chapter of First Samuel, although it makes sense to begin even earlier, with the selection of Saul as Israel's first king. Then, you can continue all the way through to David's death in the second chapter of First Kings.

Surely this story is one of the most fascinating (and instructive) ever written. More than once Satan was able to use David's powerful human emotions against him and lead David into sin. However, to the devil's consternation, more than once David also humbled himself before God, repented, asked forgiveness, and was then restored to God's favor.

As you read the whole story, you cannot help noticing one thing. Many of Satan's less-familiar efforts against David were not as direct and out in the open as they were (for example) in the more familiar story of David and Bathsheba. As he is with all of us, Satan was far too crafty and scheming to attack David from one direction only.

One short episode from David's life, the story of David and his beloved son, Absalom, illustrates Satan's technique perfectly. Satan used Jonadab, a son of David's brother and therefore Absalom's cousin, to influence Absalom's own brother (and another of David's sons), Amnon. What began with their whispered conversation eventually brought about a huge, multi-sided drama that brought much tragedy to the members of David's family. In the end it delivered one of its most devastating blows to David himself.

> ### STRAIGHT FROM THE BOOK . . .
>
> *The devil attempts to deceive us by convincing us that right is wrong and wrong is right. To be deceived is to believe a lie. The devil has absolutely no capacity to tell the full truth about anything.*

Consider the following portion of that story, taken from the Book of Second Samuel. Look up the text and fill in the blanks. The first segment comes from Second Samuel 13:3, 4.

> But Amnon had a friend whose name was Jonadab the son of Shimeah, David's brother. Now Jonadab was a very _____ man. And he said to him, "Why are you, the king's son, becoming _____ day after day? Will you not tell me?" Amnon said to him, "I love Tamar, my brother Absalom's sister" (NKJV).

Amnon and Absalom were both sons of David, but they had different mothers. Technically speaking they were half-brothers, which might help explain why Absalom's "connection" to Tamar (his full sister) turned out to be somewhat stronger than his connection to Amnon. As the old adage says, *"Blood is thicker than water"* even (or perhaps especially) in the Bible. The story continues in Second Samuel 13:5, 6 . . .

> So Jonadab said to him, "Lie down on your bed and
> _____ _____ _____ _____. And
> when your father comes to see you, say to him, 'Please let my
> sister Tamar come and give me food, and prepare the food in
> my sight, that I may see it and eat it from her hand.'" Then
> Amnon lay down and _____ _____ _____
> _____; and when the king came to see him, Amnon
> said to the king, "Please let Tamar my sister come and make
> a _____ _____ _____ for me in my sight,
> that I may eat from her hand" (NKJV).

Now David, totally unaware of what's going on, gets directly involved. (2 Sam. 13:7–9).

> And David sent home to Tamar, saying, "Now go to your
> brother Amnon's house, and prepare food for him." So Tamar
> went to her brother Amnon's house; and he was lying down.
> Then she took flour and kneaded it, made cakes in his sight,
> and baked the cakes. And she took the pan and placed them
> out before him, but he _____ _____
> _____. Then Amnon said, "Have everyone go out from
> me." And they all went out from him (NKJV).

Now that Satan has set the scene, he begins to thicken the plot (2 Sam. 13:10–14).

> Then Amnon said to Tamar, "Bring the food into the
> _____ that I may eat from your hand." And Tamar took
> the cakes which she had made, and brought them to Amnon

her brother in the bedroom. Now when she had brought them to him to eat, he took hold of her and said to her, "Come, lie with me, my sister."

But she answered him, "No, my brother, do not _____ me, for no such thing should be done in Israel. Do not do this _____ thing! And I, where could I take my shame? And as for you, you would be like one of the fools in Israel. Now therefore, please speak to the king; for he will not _____ me from you." However, he would not heed her voice; and being stronger than she, he forced her and lay with her (NKJV).

Tamar was willing to marry Amnon honorably. However, Satan's schemes often require him to push us off the right path. So it was with Amnon. And then, once he'd been nudged over the edge, almost immediately Amnon's "love" turned to a different feeling entirely. Thus, Satan's chain reaction began (2 Sam. 13:15–18).

Then Amnon hated her exceedingly, so that the _____ with which he hated her was greater than the love with which he had loved her. And Amnon said to her, "Arise, be gone!" So she said to him, "No, indeed! This evil of _____ _____ _____ is worse than the other that you did to me."

But he would not listen to her. Then he called his servant who attended him, and said, "Here! Put this woman out, away from me, and _____ the door behind her" (NKJV).

In a very real sense, Tamar's hope to marry respectably and live as a woman of standing in her ancient Hebrew community was now shattered. So, she found refuge in the only place she could (2 Sam. 13:18–22).

Now she had on a _____ _____ _____ _____, for the king's virgin daughters wore such apparel. And his servant put her out and bolted the door behind her. Then Tamar put ashes on her head, and tore her robe of many colors that was on her, and laid her hand on her head and went away _____ bitterly. And Absalom her brother said to her, "Has Amnon your brother been with you? But now hold your peace, my sister. He is your brother; do not take this thing to heart." So Tamar remained _____ in her brother Absalom's house.

But when King David heard of all these things, he was very angry. And Absalom spoke to his brother Amnon neither good nor bad. For Absalom hated Amnon, because he had forced his sister Tamar (NKJV).

The hatred Amnon so quickly developed for his sister, which resulted directly from his own sin, was nothing compared to how Absalom felt when he found out what had happened. He advised his sister to remain quiet, and even kept his own anger under wraps until the time was right, but eventually he "seized the moment" and killed Amnon in revenge.

> ### STRAIGHT FROM THE BOOK . . .
>
> *God's Word urges us to resist the devil. We are to stand firm and withstand his clever tricks that are aimed to entice us and get us off balance, trip us up, interrupt our stride, and move us to partake of things and experiences that are contrary to God's plan and purpose for our lives.*

That's not the whole story! In spite of everything, David still loved Absalom. However, Absalom fled from David's house, organized his own army, and eventually opposed David's warriors on the field of battle. And there, even though most of David's soldiers knew that David would disapprove, his most trusted general, Joab, took advantage of an incredible bit of "bad luck" that brought about Absalom's death. The story concludes in Second Samuel 18:9–15:

Then Absalom met the servants of David. Absalom rode on a mule. The mule went under the thick boughs of a great _____ tree [i.e., a small tree of the cashew family], and his _____ caught in the terebinth; so he was left hanging between heaven and earth. And the mule which was under him went on. Now a certain man saw it and told Joab, and said, "I just saw Absalom hanging in a terebinth tree!"

So Joab said to the man who told him, "You just saw him! And why did you not strike him there to the ground? I would have given you ten _____ _____ _____ and a belt."

But the man said to Joab, "Though I were to receive a thousand _____ _____ _____ in my hand, I would not raise my hand against the king's son. For in our hearing the king commanded you . . . saying, "Beware lest anyone touch the young man Absalom!' Otherwise I would have dealt falsely against my own life. For there is nothing hidden from _____ _____, and you yourself would have set yourself against me."

Then Joab said, "I cannot linger with you." And he took three spears in his hand and thrust them through Absalom's _____, while he was still alive in the midst of the terebinth tree. And ten young men who bore Joab's armor surrounded Absalom, and _____ and _____ him (NKJV).

By the time Absalom died at the hand of Joab, Satan had complicated things for David and his family to such an extent that *down* seemed to be *up* and *up* seemed to be *down*. Consider carefully the full story of Tamar, Amnon, Absalom, and David before you answer the following questions:

(1) How did Satan deceive Amnon?

_____

_____

_____

(2) What was the main lie he whispered in Amnon's ear?

_____

_____

(3) Although Tamar was innocent—and even tried to do the right thing once she had been sinned against—Satan turned her life upside down. Can you think of anything she might have done differently, to prevent any of the tragedy that followed?

_____

_____

_____

_____

(4) In what way did Absalom control his anger—at least for a while?

_____

_____

_____

_____

(5) Can you think of a wiser way in which he might have intervened, short of killing his brother?

_____

_____

_____

_____

(6) The anguish David felt at the death of his beloved son was so intense that he almost sacrificed the loyalty of his own army. Only by confronting David directly was Joab able to point out that David appeared to be grieving more for Absalom than he was rejoicing at the safety of his own people and the end of a great rebellion against his kingship. What did David then do to correct that impression?

_____

_____

_____

(7) What would Satan have preferred David do instead?

_____

_____

_____

WHAT ARE SATAN'S MAIN OBJECTIVES?

One of the anti-God arguments that non-believers often make is that God instructed the Israelites to treat the tribes that inhabited the land of Canaan before they arrived in a "bloodthirsty" way. Thus many claim that the God of the Old Testament was cruel, heartless, and indifferent to the sufferings of mankind.

For example, while the Israelites were still in the wilderness, preparing to enter Canaan, the Lord said in Exodus 23:27–30:

"I will send My fear before you, I will cause _____ among all the people to whom you come, and will make all your _____ turn their backs to you. And I will send hornets before you, which shall drive out the Hivite, the Canaanite, and the Hittite from before you. I will not drive them out from before you in one year, lest the land become _____ and the beasts of the field become too _____ for you. Little by little I will drive them out from before you, until you have increased, and you inherit the land (NKJV).

Just one verse later, God explains (Ex. 23:31–33):

". . . For I will deliver the inhabitants of the land into your hand, and you shall drive them out before you. You shall make no _____ with them, nor with their gods. They shall not dwell in your land, lest they make you _____ against Me. For if you serve their gods, it will surely be a snare to you" (NKJV).

THE LORD SAID "PLEASE"!

One highly qualified expert on the Hebrew language[1] explains that the Hebrew word that is often translated as "now," at the beginning of the Lord's instruction to Abraham about sacrificing his son, Isaac, should actually be translated, in that situation, as "please." If you make that substitution in Genesis 22:2 (as in "Take, now, your son, your only son Isaac, whom you love . . ."), instead of saying "Take now" the Lord is saying "Take, please." What a different view of God that little insight provides!

In other words, God knew how His people could be pulled away from Him by Satan, one small step at a time. In fact, many years before God spoke these specific words Satan had already taken notice and begun to act accordingly. Satan's objectives have always been the same:

(A) To draw us away from God

(B) To thwart us in pursuing God's purpose and plan for our lives.

(C) To deny God the glory, honor, and praise due Him.

(D) To destroy us—literally and eternally.

✎ Write (or indicate by their reference letters) all of the above objectives that you believe Satan was attempting to achieve in each of the following Scripture passages.

(1) Genesis 3:1–4

_____

_____

_____

(2) Genesis 28:8, 9

_____

_____

_____

(3) Matthew 4:1–11

_____

_____

_____

(4) Matthew 9:34

_____

_____

_____

(5) Luke 1:18–20

_____

_____

_____

(6) Luke 5:30

_____

_____

_____

⋘ FOR HIS EYES ONLY ⋙

God has clearly placed certain limitations on Satan's power. Even so, as we have seen, Satan can still . . .

(1) Destroy the quality of our lives by sending sickness and injury our way.

(2) Attack our peace and joy by stirring up trouble.

(3) Use unbelievers or weak believers to harm us physically.

(4) Bring confusion, anger, and frustration into situations and relationships.

⋘Write a short expression of gratitude to God, _for His eyes only_, in which you recount one major incident in your life in which ▼

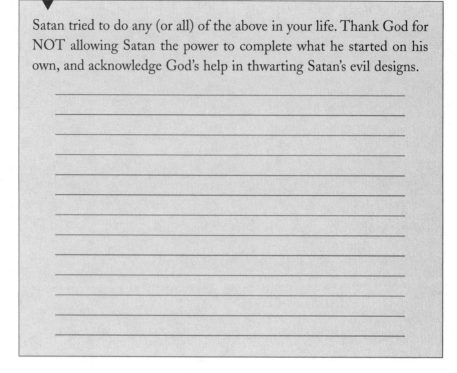

Satan tried to do any (or all) of the above in your life. Thank God for NOT allowing Satan the power to complete what he started on his own, and acknowledge God's help in thwarting Satan's evil designs.

_____

_____

_____

_____

_____

_____

_____

_____

_____

_____

_____

_____

_____

WE CANNOT DEFEAT SATAN IN OUR OWN STRENGTH

Many verses in the Bible illustrate that we cannot defeat Satan in our own strength. Consider just two, one that lays out the ageless problem that affects all mankind and one that lays out the glorious solution God has provided:

While they promise them liberty, they themselves are slaves of corruption; for by whom a person is overcome, by him also he is brought into bondage (2 Pet. 2:19, NKJV).

You are of God, little children, and have overcome them, because He who is in you is greater than he who is in the world. They [Note: "They" = false teachers, although this could also apply to any of Satan's helpers] are of the world. Therefore they speak as of the world, and the world hears them. We are of God. He who knows God hears us; he who is not of God does not hear us. By this we know the spirit of truth and the spirit of error (1 John 4:4, 5, NKJV).

WORDS TO REMEMBER . . .

LORD, You have heard the desire of the humble; You will prepare their heart; You will cause Your ear to hear, To do justice to the fatherless and the oppressed, That the man of the earth may oppress no more (Ps. 10:17, 18, NKJV).

CLOSING PRAYER . . .

Our Father, help us never to forget the vast differences between the good things You bring into our lives and the evil things Satan would have us embrace. Keep us mindful of Your grace and Your strength, and help us be faithful to rely on You in all things.

In Jesus' name, Amen.

3

—◦◦◦—

THE OUTCOME OF THE BATTLE

The following story is a little long, but it makes a worthwhile point.

Recently, the wife of one of my editors was scheduled to leave on an important trip early in the morning. She would be gone two weeks, conducting a workshop for school teachers in a distant city. Her notebooks were assembled; her bags packed; her tickets purchased; her rooms set aside; her rental car reserved. She had even gone to the ATM machine to extract $200 in case she needed last-minute supplies.

That evening, since everything seemed to be in perfect order, she and her husband decided to relax by watching a video. She went to the rental store, made her selection, and returned home.

An hour later, as they were finishing dinner, she reached for her purse to check on something and discovered that her billfold was missing. "Oh no!" she said. "I had my plane tickets in there, my credit cards, all my traveling money! We have to find it!"

First they searched the house and the car, to no avail. Nothing. Nowhere. So her husband jumped into the car and raced back to the video store. "Maybe you dropped it on the pavement, or left it on the counter," he shouted as he ran out, without even pausing to put on his shoes. "I've got to get there before someone else spots it, in case it's lying in the open!"

The moment he arrived he jumped out and began searching the pavement. All the spaces were full, so he found himself poking frantically under the cars that were now "in the way." Finally he went into the store, talked to all the clerks, walked every aisle, and tried to look on every shelf.

BACK HOME AGAIN . . .

Nothing. At last he got back in the car and drove home. On the way his mind worked overtime. They needed the fee his wife would collect. Their income had been down recently, but now they were trapped—the minute he got home he'd have to cancel all their credit cards. And the $300 in cash was clearly gone—no way they could do anything to get that back.

Worse yet, though her airplane tickets might be replaceable she couldn't collect her rental car or pay for her room without any ID. What could they possibly do?

For the last few blocks the young man finally began to pray. "Lord, we have always trusted You. We know that somehow You always take care of us. Right now we're in big trouble—we need help!"

It would be nice to claim that he felt instant relief, but that's not what happened. In a few moments he drove into the garage and turned off the engine, his mind still racing. Absent-mindedly, he picked up the video his wife had rented, still lying on the front seat on top of a section of yesterday's newspaper. Crumpling the paper in one hand as he walked, he set the video on the shelf above the trash can, well above eye level, to free his other hand so he could take the top off the can. When he reached back up to pick up the video, his hand touched something else lying next to it. Something smooth and leathery. A billfold!

"Honey! Is this it?" he shouted as he charged into the house. Sure enough, it was, and everything was there. Suddenly, his wife knew exactly what had happened.

She had also thrown away some trash as she came inside, setting her purse on the same shelf to free her other hand. The purse had

Not a Coincidence at All . . .

It has become fashionable, in recent years, to mock the belief that God had a hand in the founding of our nation. Nonetheless, the evidence is overwhelming to those who are willing to look at it objectively, with no preconceptions and no axe to grind. God is not a God of coincidences; He is a God of planning and purpose.

Not surprisingly, even America's discovery by Christopher Columbus (yes, I know; he actually landed on an island not far from Cuba—but his expedition brought about the flood of exploration that followed) came at the end of an excruciating battle with doubt and fatigue. Columbus truly believed he was on a mission from God, but just days before he and his sailors sighted land he was almost forced by his companions to give up and return to Portugal. By that time even he was wracked with doubt; they had already sailed hundreds of miles farther than any European had ever gone before, and the members of his crew were terrified that they would soon be "too far gone" ever to return.

How many times, in how many lives, has God asked us to hold the course just a few more hours, a few more miles . . . at which point He always steps in and makes up the difference.

slipped open, the billfold had slid out, and she simply hadn't missed it until later. At once they both realized the same thing.

Only God could have led that young husband to do almost exactly what his wife had done when she arrived home, to put him in exactly the right place. Only God could have directed his hand to go where his eye could not, to exactly the right spot to land on what they'd lost.

Straight from the Book . . .

If you perceive that you are in control of your life and any particular situation, you are in trouble. Why? Because you can't possibly control everything in life or have the wisdom to know what to do in every situation for all people involved.

DIRECT INTERVENTION

That was a long story, but I believe it shows how God can directly intervene and cancel out even the most insidious efforts Satan makes to introduce chaos and disaster into our lives.

However, many such stories, even though they end every bit as well, cannot be so neatly tied up into one-hour or even one-day events.

FOR DEEPER CONSIDERATION . . .

All believers have success stories to tell! If you are part of a study group, ask members to tell a story about how God countered one of Satan's attempts to disrupt their life.

GOD IS ALWAYS IN CONTROL

Sometimes it takes years for the plans of God to bring about a final outcome; sometimes the detailed schemes of Satan also take years to play themselves out and to completely unravel or disintegrate.

Let's consider the familiar story of Joseph and his brothers, but this time, let's take it one major event at a time. Read the following biblical passages and then answer the questions. At the end we'll pull it all together.

✎ **Read Genesis 37:2–11.**

(1) What was the gift that caused jealousy—and even hatred—among the sons of Jacob?

_____

_____

_____

_____

(2) Who was the recipient of that gift? The object of that hatred? What character trait did he apparently have, which might have worked against him—at least in the short term?

_____

_____

_____

_____

(3) What were the two prophetic dreams that he recounted to his brothers?

_____

_____

_____

_____

Read Genesis 37:12–36.

(1) What sin did Joseph's brothers originally plot against Joseph?

_____

_____

_____

_____

(2) Why did they not carry out their original plans? What one person was most responsible, at this point, for sparing Joseph's life?

_____

_____

_____

_____

Read Genesis 39 (You'll love the plot!).

(1) Name three of Joseph's positive traits, which justified the responsibility and trust Potiphar gave him.

_____

_____

_____

(2) Which of Joseph's physical qualities did Satan use against him via Potiphar's wife?

_____

_____

_____

(3) What punishment did Joseph suffer as a result?

_____

_____

_____

_____

STRAIGHT FROM THE BOOK . . .

Too many people seem to think that God and Satan are in a tug-of-war, one pulling one way toward good and the other pulling in the opposite direction toward evil. While God and Satan are opponents, they are not equals. Satan is a created being, a finite creature. God is the infinite Creator. There's no comparison in their power, majesty, or glory.

Now I want to skip ahead to the most significant part of the story. I would certainly encourage you to read everything in between, which covers . . .

How Joseph's God-given ability to interpret dreams, first demonstrated in prison, brought him to Pharaoh's attention.

How his talents as an honest man, an organizer, and a planner eventually made him rich, powerful, and famous throughout the land.

How those same talents, combined with the insights God gave him, saved thousands of lives.

How he saved his brothers and their father, too, in spite of what had been done to him.

Let's go to the very end of Genesis, after Jacob has died. Joseph's brothers are terrified that, without their father's calming influence, Joseph will take revenge on them for what they did to him years before. However, what does Joseph do? (Gen. 50:19–21):

Joseph said to them, "Do not be afraid, for am I in the place of God? But as for you, you meant _____ against me; but God meant it for _____, in order to bring it about as it is this day, to save many people alive. Now therefore, do not be afraid; I will _____ for you and your little ones." And he _____ them and spoke _____ to them (NKJV).

Many lessons can be drawn from this passage. However, the lesson we are most concerned with at this point is how God dealt with Satan at every turn, canceling Satan's evil plans and bringing about His own divine purposes. Perhaps the easiest way to understand this concept is to make a table, listing the major events in the story of Joseph, followed by what Satan hoped to achieve, then considering God's purpose for allowing those same circumstances. The third row is filled out for you to help you get started.

Event or Circumstance	Considering Satan's Intent	Considering God's Purpose
Jacob gives Joseph the coat of many colors.		
Joseph dreams dreams and interprets them for his brothers.		
Joseph's brothers sell him to the slave traders.	To separate Joseph from his family and perhaps to kill him	To position Joseph in Egypt, where he will be needed later

The slave traders sell Joseph to Potiphar, as a slave.		
Joseph encounters Potiphar's wife, who falsely accuses him.		
Joseph goes to prison.		
Joseph interprets dreams for the cup-bearer and the baker.		
Joseph interprets Pharaoh's dreams.		
Joseph rises to second-in-command over all Egypt.		
Joseph meets his brothers again.		
Joseph meets his brothers a second time.		
The entire life story of Joseph		

BECAUSE GOD IS IN CONTROL . . .

Certain things are always true with respect to each attack of the devil:

▷ Each attack is limited in scope.

▷ Each attack is limited in duration.

▷ The good that God brings about, from each attack, will be greater than the severity of the attack itself.

▷ The result that God will bring about will strike a blow against the devil, bring about eternal benefit to God's children, and bring glory to God.

✎ Given these truths, consider how they apply to each separate attack that Satan launched against Joseph.

(1) Was each one limited in scope?

_____

_____

(2) Was each one limited in duration?

_____

_____

(3) How would you measure the good God brought about vs. the severity of the evil Satan planned?

_____

_____

(4) Did all these attacks, taken together, bring about eternal benefit to God's children and bring Him glory, too?

_____

_____

STRAIGHT FROM THE BOOK . . .

Whenever the devil strikes us, we can take heart that God has a purpose in allowing the devil to act. The purpose is a divine one that we may not understand but that, nonetheless, is for our good or the good of others.

YOU CAN ALWAYS COUNT ON THREE MORE THINGS!

#1: God will always help you. Fill in the blanks for these examples—just two among many more. First, read the words of Jacob in Genesis 49:25, blessing his sons before he died:

By the God of your father who will _____ you, and by the Almighty who will _____ you with _____ of heaven above, blessings of the deep that lies beneath, blessings of the breasts and of the womb (NKJV).

Next, read the words of Paul in Acts 26:22, testifying before King Agrippa:

Therefore, having obtained _____ from God, to this day I stand, witnessing both to small and great, saying no other things than those which the prophets and Moses said would come—(NKJV).

What is the common testimony of these two passages? What is that testimony based on?

_____

_____

_____

_____

_____

≪≋▷**#2:** No temptation or crisis will last forever.

≪≋▷**#3:** Each one will make you stronger in spirit.

Jesus was tempted, intensively, for exactly 40 days. After Noah entered the ark it rained for exactly 40 days. However, this does not mean that every crisis in your life will last for exactly 40 days!

(1) What is the longest duration of a major crisis you have experienced?

_____

_____

(2) Did the Lord give you the strength to endure?

_____

_____

_____

(3) If not, did you ask (or have you asked) Him to do so?

_____

_____

_____

Would you do so now?

AND MORE EXAMPLES . . .

Finally, consider three more verses that reinforce all that we have studied up to this point:

John 15:2
Every branch in Me that does not bear fruit He takes away; and every branch that bears fruit He prunes, that it may bear more fruit.

Hebrews 12:10–11

For they indeed for a few days chastened us as seemed best to them, but He for our profit, that we may be partakers of His holiness.

Now no chastening seems to be joyful for the present, but painful; nevertheless, afterward it yields the peaceable fruit of righteousness to those who have been trained by it.

The outcome of the battle is settled even before the battle begins, as long as we have the Lord in our hearts.

WORDS TO REMEMBER . . .

This most beloved psalm of David's is well-worth memorizing. It is also one of the Bible's most powerful testimonies to the power of God to protect and sustain us through all our lives:

I will lift up my eyes to the hills— From whence comes my help? My help comes from the LORD, Who made heaven and earth. He will not allow your foot to be moved; He who keeps you will not slumber. Behold, He who keeps Israel Shall neither slumber nor sleep. The LORD is your keeper; The LORD is your shade at your right hand. The sun shall not strike you by day, Nor the moon by night. The LORD shall preserve you from all evil; He shall preserve your soul. The LORD shall preserve your going out and your coming in From this time forth, and even forevermore (Psalm 121, NKJV).

CLOSING PRAYER . . .

Our Father, we pray that You would grant us the strength we need for each of the crises we face here on Earth. Strengthen our faith that we may trust in You, remember Your promises, and depend on Your grace. May we praise Your name in all things and glorify You at every moment.

In Jesus' name, Amen.

4

―ᴧᴧ―

THE ENEMY'S SNARES

No one who lived in biblical times would have difficulty understanding the word "snare." In five of the most popular translations of the Bible it appears 34 times in one, 57 times in another, and somewhere in between in each of the others. This includes the *New King James Version*, where it appears 45 times.

It also occurs eight or nine times more often in the Old Testament than the New for two obvious reasons. First, the Old Testament (plus direct quotations from it in the New Testament) accounts for about 80 percent of the Bible. I'm not a mathematician, but if everything else were equal it seems to me that the four-times-longer portion should therefore contain the word snare at a 4-to-1 ratio.

Perhaps there is a second reason. In the Old Testament God raised up His chosen people and set them on a new course—one on which no group of people on Earth had ever traveled with as much direct guidance from Him. By their very nature the historical books and prophetic writings of the Old Testament contain a greater percentage of warnings about what the Lord's followers should avoid. Thus the word *snare* comes into play.

FOR DEEPER CONSIDERATION . . .

The snare of associating too closely with those who worship false gods, or with those who oppose God in various other ways, is the snare most often warned against in the Bible. Paul also reinforced that concept in Second Corinthians 6:17: "Therefore, 'Come out from among them and be separate,' says the Lord. Do not touch what is unclean, and I will receive you.'"

As Christians, what are we to do with that concept? Why was the Lord so concerned about His people falling in with non-Christian influences? Aren't we to be "strong in the Lord" and able to withstand the enemy's darts in all times and places?

_____

_____

_____

_____

_____

_____

_____

_____

_____

"Snare" Is Often Used in Metaphors

Many of those warnings are what linguists would call metaphorical. In other words, they teach a larger truth by illustrating it with a smaller one that's easier to understand. And "easier to understand" means that the illustrations have to involve real things that real people meet in real life.

Certainly, snares were an everyday part of life for many Old Testament people. Even today, if too many forest creatures live in a populated area, forest rangers will use some combination of trickery and traps to *ensnare* them and move them to other places.

But no man could be cleverer, for a longer time, than Satan. He's been using snares of all kinds since he first found himself thrown out of heaven. Let's look at biblical examples of some of the snares Satan began using centuries ago—and still uses today.

THE SNARE OF DEBATE

✎ Fill in the blanks in this passage, found in Numbers 16:1–3.

> Now Korah the son of Izhar, the son of Kohath, the son of Levi, with Dathan and Abiram the sons of Eliab, and On the son of Peleth, sons of Reuben, took men; and they rose up before Moses with some of the children of Israel, two hundred and fifty _____ of the congregation, representatives of the congregation, men of _____. They gathered together against Moses and Aaron, and said to them, "You take too much upon yourselves, for all the congregation is _____, every one of them, and the LORD is among them. Why then do you _____ yourselves above the _____ of the LORD?" (NKJV)

(1) Describe the snare Satan attempted to use against Moses while the Israelites were encamped in the wilderness?

_____

_____

_____

_____

_____

(2) What would have been the most likely result if Moses had taken the bait and begun to argue with Korah?

_____

_____

_____

_____

_____

(3) What did Moses do instead, as recounted in Numbers 16:4–7?

So when Moses heard it, he fell on his face; and he spoke to Korah and all his company, saying, "Tomorrow morning the LORD will show who is His and who is holy, and will cause him to come near to Him. That one whom He _____ He will cause to come near to Him. Do this: Take censers [vessels for burning incense], Korah and all your company; put fire in them and put incense in them before the LORD tomorrow, and it shall be that the man whom the LORD chooses is the _____ one. You take too much upon yourselves, you sons of Levi!" (NKJV)

_____

_____

_____

_____

I italicized Korah's ancestry in the Numbers 16:1–3 passage, to remind us that Korah came from the tribe of Levi. Therefore, he was already among those who were commissioned by God to work in the temple. He wanted more, however; even though he was not a son of Aaron, he wanted to be part of the official priesthood as well. It sounds like He even felt that he should have Moses' job! And so he took the reckless step of challenging Moses and Aaron, the leaders chosen by God.

However, rather than falling for Satan's snare and entering into a debate, Moses fell on his face in front of God before he even responded to Korah. And when he did speak he said exactly what God told him to say. Then he got out of the way and let God take charge and handle the matter for him!

STRAIGHT FROM THE BOOK . . .

Satan's Lie #1: *Saved people don't sin. Furthermore, they don't have any desire to sin, and they aren't tempted. The truth is that saved people do sin from time to time. They still are human and live in fleshly bodies with fleshly desires. Every person is tempted.*

Numbers 16:8–35 tells what happened next. For now, let's consider how often any of us follow the same procedure Moses followed.

On the following lines, tell the story of a time when you were drawn into an argument that did not solve a problem—preferably some time ago so you can be more objective. Whether the argument started from something you did or something that was done to you is really not important. First, tell what happened. Then, tell what might have happened if you'd turned the matter over to God in the very beginning.

What actually happened:

_____

_____

_____

_____

_____

_____

What could have happened if God had been in charge:

_____

_____

_____

_____

_____

_____

THE SNARE OF DIVISION

A young man I once knew worked in a warehouse, supervising a large crew of men and women charged with maintaining order and shipping products on time. One day he passed by one of his female employees, sitting on the concrete floor, straightening out the contents of a bin full of electronic parts. "Wow—that's gotta' be a cold place to sit!" he said, smiling, as he passed.

Two days later he was called into the company office to answer a formal complaint of sexual harassment. He had been accused of making an inappropriate comment to a female employee. At first he was astonished; then scared; then angry that both his words and his intent could have been so completely misrepresented.

Eventually, his explanation of what he had actually said, backed up by a perfect work record and a solid reputation, prevailed over the false accusations, and he was cleared of any wrongdoing. However, by that time his entire crew had chosen sides, and the division he had to deal with from that moment onward could simply never be resolved. He left the company soon after.

What's the point? Well, this is a classic example of one of Satan's more familiar techniques—to ensnare us by false accusations, creating false divisions among us, followed by what often becomes our complete inability to function in a normal way.

✎Read the following verses and notice the underlined word that appears in all of them. Then answer the questions at the end:

(1) Matthew 12:10
And behold, there was a man who had a withered hand. And they asked Him, saying, "Is it lawful to heal on the Sabbath?"—that they might <u>accuse</u> Him (NKJV).

(2) Mark 3:2
And they watched Him closely, whether He would heal him on the Sabbath, so that they might <u>accuse</u> Him (NKJV).

(3) Mark 15:4
Then Pilate asked Him again, saying, "Do You answer nothing? See how many things they <u>testify</u> against You!" [i.e., meaning that they accused Him] (NKJV)

(4) Luke 11:54
lying in wait for Him, and seeking to catch Him in something He might say, that they might <u>accuse</u> Him (NKJV).

(5) Luke 23:2

And they began to <u>accuse</u> Him, saying, "We found this fellow perverting the nation, and forbidding to pay taxes to Caesar, saying that He Himself is Christ, a King" (NKJV).

(6) Luke 23:14

said to them, "You have brought this Man to me, as one who misleads the people. And indeed, having examined Him in your presence, I have found no fault in this Man concerning those things of which you <u>accuse</u> Him (NKJV).

(7) John 8:6

This they said, testing Him, that they might have something of which to <u>accuse</u> Him. But Jesus stooped down and wrote on the ground with His finger, as though He did not hear (NKJV).

These examples all detail the actions of those who were determined to find fault with our Savior, no matter what. Over and over again, as repeated in all four Gospels, they falsely accused Jesus whenever they had the slightest chance, and at the end they purposely created their own opportunities.

What was Jesus' response? Look up each of these passages and read them again in context, perhaps three verses before and three verses after. Then indicate, on the numbered lines below, what Jesus did in each case. Use the column of lines on the left, called "Before Trial," if the incident happened before He went on trial for His life. Use the column on the right, called "At Trial," if it happened during or at His trial.

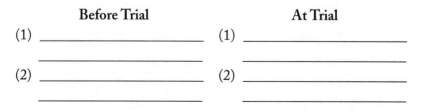

Before Trial	**At Trial**
(1) _____	(1) _____
_____	_____
(2) _____	(2) _____
_____	_____

(3) _____   (3) _____

_____   _____

(4) _____   (4) _____

_____   _____

(5) _____   (5) _____

_____   _____

(6) _____   (6) _____

_____   _____

(7) _____   (7) _____

_____   _____

STRAIGHT FROM THE BOOK . . .

Satan's Lie #2: *Some sins are beyond forgiveness—either because the sins are so great in magnitude or because they are repeated so often. God's Word tells us that when we confess our sins to God, He is faithful in forgiving our sins and cleansing us from all unrighteousness. (See 1 John 1:9.) God's mercy and patience with us are beyond measure.*

Do you see a pattern here? In some of the earlier examples—for example, when he was first accused of breaking the law by healing on the Sabbath—Jesus responded by pointing out the hypocrisy of His accusers. By way of teaching all of us down through the generations, He explained how they had perverted God's Law and changed it into man's law.

By doing that they could then appoint themselves as authorities over other people.

On the other hand, near the end of His life, when He was doing His Father's will by purposely laying down His life for our sins, Jesus didn't even bother to defend Himself.

(1) Given those examples, are there ever times when we should be silent in the face of false accusations?

_____

_____

(2) Are there other times when we should respond?

_____

_____

(3) If so, can you name some possibilities?

_____

_____

(4) In any such case, what is the one thing we should always avoid?

_____

_____

FOR DEEPER CONSIDERATION . . .

One of the clearest examples of someone being snared by the devil and tricked into defying God directly was Jacob's twin brother, Esau. When Jacob stole the blessing of the firstborn from Esau, the devil introduced a major division within the family. Jacob went away to a distant land to find a wife. He stayed there many years and had to withstand major deceptions from his uncle Laban. Some commentators say that Jacob's trials were punishment for leaping ahead of God and pursuing the birthright (which God clearly wanted Him to have) with his mother's help, rather than allowing God to work it out in His own perfect way.

Esau's response, however, was more direct and far more damaging to himself in the long run. As told in Genesis 28:6–9, Esau went out and deliberately married Canaanite wives who worshiped false idols, to spite his father and to express his anger at losing the birthright (which legally should have been his since he was the firstborn). Of course, the negative effects of such marriages, which would tend to pull Esau farther and farther away from the true God, were heavily visited upon him. Perhaps the old expression about "cutting off your nose to spite your face" was first applied to Esau.

If you are part of a group, ask if anyone can give a real-life situation which resembles Esau's actions. Consider your community or your state. Is anything of that kind going on right now in public life?

▼

▼ _____

_____

_____

_____

_____

_____

_____

_____

_____

_____

_____

_____

_____

_____

_____

THE SNARE OF DOUBT

Satan knows that if he can make us doubt the truth of God's Word or wonder about our personal relationships with Him, he can undermine our walk with the Lord and perhaps even knock us off the path.

Perhaps the most telling response to issues of doubt raised by the devil can be found in these familiar words of Jesus. After He withered the fruitless fig tree, His disciples wondered how it could have happened so quickly. Jesus responded in Matthew 21:21:

So Jesus answered and said to them, "Assuredly, I say to you, if you have _____ and do not _____, you will not only do what was done to the fig tree, but also if you say to this _____, 'Be removed and be cast into the sea,' it will be done (NKJV).

From this verse it is clear that doubt has no legitimate place in our lives. Yet it is equally clear that doubts can assail us at any time—sometimes Satan simply will not give us a rest! In general, he most often brings doubts about the truth of God's Word (already proven true many times over) and about our own relationships with Him.

The second of these is usually the most difficult to deal with unless we fortify ourselves with God's Word. Fortunately, God has given us literally dozens and dozens of promises about our salvation—and He has proven over and over again that He has neither lied nor changed. Consider just ten of the most familiar, among dozens of equally powerful, equally clear examples we could cite.

> ### Straight from the Book . . .
>
> Satan's Lie #3: *God gets weary of people who sin and repent repeatedly, and He eventually stops forgiving their sins. The truth is that God may chastise us and discipline us when we develop a habit of sinning, but God does not abandon us or cease to forgive us. He continues to prod us toward the way of righteousness so that we will make right choices and reap godly rewards.*

✐Matthew 5:11, 12

Blessed are you when they revile and persecute you, and say all kinds of evil against you falsely for My sake. Rejoice and be exceedingly glad, for great is your reward in heaven, for so they persecuted the prophets who were before you (NKJV).

✐Matthew 17:20

So Jesus said to them, "Because of your unbelief; for assuredly, I say to you, if you have faith as a mustard seed, you will say to this mountain, 'Move from here to there,' and it will move; and nothing will be impossible for you (NKJV).

✐Romans 8:28

And we know that all things work together for good to those who love God, to those who are the called according to His purpose (NKJV).

✎▷**Romans 8:31**

What then shall we say to these things? If God is for us, who can be against us? (NKJV)

✎▷**Philippians 4:13**

I can do all things through Christ who strengthens me (NKJV).

✎▷**2 Timothy 2:13**

If we are faithless, He remains faithful; He cannot deny Himself (NKJV).

✎▷**2 Timothy 2:19**

Nevertheless the solid foundation of God stands, having this seal: "The Lord knows those who are His . . ." (NKJV).

✎▷**2 Peter 3:9**

The Lord is not slack concerning His promise, as some count slackness, but is longsuffering toward us, not willing that any should perish but that all should come to repentance (NKJV).

✎▷**Revelation 3:21**

To him who overcomes I will grant to sit with Me on My throne, as I also overcame and sat down with My Father on His throne (NKJV).

✎▷**Revelation 21:7**

He who overcomes shall inherit all things, and I will be his God and he shall be My son (NKJV).

All these verses repeat two or three basic ideas, or themes, with respect to our relationship to God and His to us. Can you identify those themes?

_____

GOD'S TRUTH IS THE ANTIDOTE FOR DECEPTION

These and other verses demonstrate that God's own Word—the Truth He has given us directly through writers that He inspired by the Holy Spirit—is the best antidote against Satan's deceptions. Satan's snares are more detectable if we prepare and defend ourselves by regular study of God's Word.

No lie can stand for long against the truth. This is especially true of Satan's pathetic falsehoods, for they are directly refuted by the ultimate source of Truth.

WORDS TO REMEMBER . . .

. . . But we urge you, brethren, that . . . you also aspire to lead a quiet life, to mind your own business, and to work with your own hands, as we commanded you, that you may walk properly toward those who are outside, and that you may lack nothing (1 Thess. 4:10–12, NKJV).

CLOSING PRAYER . . .

Our Father, teach us to be wary of Satan's snares; teach us, instead, to seek Your face, to lean on You, to ask Your help, and to give ourselves into Your keeping at all times. May we depend always and forever on Your arms of protection.

In Jesus' name, Amen.

> ⤜⤙   FOR HIS EYES ONLY . . .   ⤜⤙
>
> *Write a private note to God, about your greatest, most nagging doubt about Him, about His plan of salvation, or about your own spiritual condition that you can remember having in your entire life. Explain to Him why you doubted in the first place. Detail the deceptions Satan confused you with. Look carefully at all the aspects of that entire situation and lay them all out as clearly as you can before God. Then thank Him for helping you overcome a major snare, sent straight from the devil, and praise Him for His grace!*
>
> *When you have finished thanking and praising Him, ask Him to continue guiding and protecting you from any snares that might come in the future.*
>
> _____
>
> _____
>
> _____
>
> _____
>
> _____
>
> _____
>
> _____
>
> _____
>
> _____
>
> _____
>
> _____

STRAIGHT FROM THE BOOK . . .

What Satan says to the unbeliever about Jesus often sounds appealing because it plays on what the unbeliever already wants to believe and the way the unbeliever already wants to live.

5

—⁓—

LEARNING TO DISCERN

DEDUCTION OR DISCERNMENT?

When Sherlock Holmes notes that the man in front of him has a trace of greenish slime on his shoe, a fleck of red under his fingernail, and an empty leather sheath on his belt, he might suspect instantly that—if the same man weren't the killer—at the very least he probably knows *something* about the demise of the dead girl now lying in the peat moss bog with a hunting knife in her back.

However, that knowledge is not a product of discernment. It's the result of careful observation and inferential reasoning. As Holmes himself would say, it's simply an elementary deduction.

Likewise, when a modern detective uses DNA sampling to identify the source of a blond hair from a dead man's collar, then identifies the brand of lipstick on the man's cheek and notes that the woman who lost the first also wore the second, he should know instantly that—even though the woman might not know a .45-caliber handgun from a Turkish meat loaf—she probably knows *something* about how a bullet from a gun of the above size found its way into the man's body.

However, whatever the detective learns from his examination of the evidence, he is not *discerning* anything. He is *deducing*, based on physical facts that are readily observable to the trained eye—especially one that's backed up by electron microscopes and samples of all known lip glosses.

On a more domestic level, when a modern mother finds cookie crumbs in the kitchen, hears a breath sprayer being used, and then smells cigarette smoke on her 12-year-old son's shirt when he comes out of the bathroom, she doesn't even need any scientific gadgetry to know three things. *First*, that her son has probably been smoking; *second*, that he ate cookies to cover up the scent; and *third*, that he tried to cover himself even more by adding a breath spray as well. The mother recognizes all the clues because she knows her son and has learned some things from experience.

Once again, this mother is not *discerning* anything. She is simply reaching an obvious conclusion by *deductive reasoning*.

Far too many people speak of discernment when they really mean deduction, or speak of discernment as though it were a spiritual tool reserved for a few chosen people—and could not be developed or used by anyone else.

Consider the main difference: *Deduction* is of the mind; *discernment* is of the spirit.

Which one will serve you better in your walk with the Lord and your fight against evil? Don't answer too quickly—consider a few biblical examples first!

STRAIGHT FROM THE BOOK . . .

We hear countless voices in a given day—some of them come from people who work with us or live with us or around us; some of the voices are in the media; some of the "voices" are in our memories or in our minds. Do you know the sound of God's voice?

THE BIBLE SHOWS US THE DIFFERENCE

Consider a story we worked with back in chapter 1—that of Solomon, the two women, and the baby they both claimed as their own, as told in First Kings 3:16–27. If you're not sure of the details, reread the passage. Then answer the following questions:

(1) Did Solomon deduce or discern the identity of the true mother? Either way, what did he have to know about human nature in general, and about mothers in particular?

_____

_____

_____

_____

(2) What part did Solomon's wisdom play in the story?

_____

_____

_____

_____

Now jump ahead to one of the New Testament passages we also worked with in chapter 1—that of Ananias and Sapphira, the husband and wife who both perished for lying about their financial assets, as told in Acts 5:1–5. Focus on verse 3: "But Peter said, 'Ananias, why has Satan filled your heart to lie to the Holy Spirit and keep back part of the price of the land for yourself?'"

(1) How did Peter know Ananias was lying—deduction or discernment?

_____

_____

_____

_____

(2) Here's the tricky question again: what part did Peter's personal mental ability play in the story?

_____

_____

_____

_____

Turn to one last example, found in Acts 16:16–19, and fill in the blanks.

> Now it happened, as we went to _____, that a certain slave girl possessed with a spirit of _____ met us, who brought her masters much profit by fortune-telling. This girl followed Paul and us, and cried out, saying, "These men are the _____ of the Most High God, who _____ to us the way of salvation." And this she did for many days.
>
> But Paul, greatly annoyed, turned and said to the spirit, "I command you in the name of Jesus Christ to come out of her." And he came out that very hour (NKJV).

(1) How did Paul know that the slave girl was possessed by a spirit? Did he know it by deduction or discernment?

_____

_____

_____

_____

(2) Whatever your answer, why do you believe it's correct?

_____

_____

_____

_____

DISCERNMENT BETWEEN GOOD AND EVIL

Now it's confession time. The distinction I've tried to make between *deduce* and *discern* is important (look up both words in the dictionary if you're not convinced), but I believe that we actually need to be able to do both. Because, in real life it's often hard to tell where one stops and the other begins. They *must* work together.

A MAN OF LIMITED DISCERNMENT . . .

To read about a man of God who somehow did not seem to have the discernment he should have had, read First Samuel 13:1–25. This is an amazing story, with such a sad ending that many people have wondered why it is even in the Bible! I believe it is there to demonstrate how importance it is to discern the difference between a direct word from God and a contrary word from man. One leads to life. The other leads to death—in this case, in a very literal way.

Please know that your walk with the Lord is not about ultra-fine, legalistic distinctions; it's about making sure that you are walking closely enough with Him to know that *His* input is a *regular, constant, absolutely essential part* of every decision you make.

You need to bring all your mental faculties to bear on every situation in your life. Ultimately it's even more important to bring God into the equation to help you discern the crucial differences between:

STRAIGHT FROM THE BOOK . . .

To determine if it truly is the Lord who is speaking to you, you need to check the message against God's Word—and not just against one isolated verse that may seem to verify or confirm what you want the message to be. You need to weigh the message you are receiving from God against the whole of God's truth.

▷ Good and evil

▷ Reality and illusion

▷ Good and best

▷ Your desires and God's desires

REALITY AND ILLUSION

We've already shown how various biblical characters spotted the difference between good and evil, so let's talk about reality and illusion. Turn to Matthew 14:25–32. This familiar story depicts Peter's walking on the water, imitating Jesus. Read the story for yourself and then answer the questions.

(1) Was Jesus' walking on the water a reality or an illusion?

_____

_____

_____

(2) What about Peter's walking on the water—did he really do it, or was it an illusion?

_____

_____

_____

(3) Why did Peter almost drown?

_____

_____

_____

(4) What was the one reality that Peter should have hung on to?

_____

_____

_____

(5) What part did Peter's discernment play in all this?

_____

_____

_____

GOOD AND BEST

Now turn to First Samuel 16:1–13 and read the story of Samuel's visit to Jesse and his eight sons. Samuel went reluctantly, only at God's command, to anoint the next king of Israel. The Lord's choice would eventually fall on Saul. Read the passage and then answer the following questions.

STRAIGHT FROM THE BOOK...

God does not desire that any person live a so-so, average life. He desires for every person to live an excellent life—morally excellent, spiritually excellent, and relationally excellent.

(1) How did Samuel feel about God's refusal to approve any of Jesse's first seven sons?

_____

_____

_____

(2) If he'd had his own way, who do you think Samuel might have chosen?

_____

_____

_____

_____

(3) What was God's position in the matter—who did He insist be the one anointed, and why?

_____

_____

_____

_____

(4) Why did Samuel fail, at first, to discern the Lord's true intent?

_____

_____

_____

_____

YOUR DESIRES AND GOD'S DESIRES

God always wants the very best for each of His followers, both *for* them and *from* them. Unfortunately, many of us would be content with far less if we could have things our own way, including some of the greatest figures in history.

For example, Moses is often hailed as the greatest of the Children of Israel's leaders, but he was not always a willing hero. When God first called him, he had other ideas, and he contended with God more than once over *whether* and *how* he would serve. The following passage narrates one example of what might have seemed to Moses like a typical conversation between himself and God:

> Then Moses said to the LORD, "O my Lord, I am not eloquent, neither before nor since You have spoken to Your servant; but I am slow of speech and slow of tongue."
>
> So the LORD said to him, "Who has made man's mouth? Or who makes the mute, the deaf, the seeing, or the blind? Have not I, the LORD? Now therefore, go, and I will be with your mouth and teach you what you shall say."
>
> But he said, "O my Lord, please send by the hand of whomever else You may send."
>
> So the anger of the LORD was kindled against Moses, and He said: "Is not Aaron the Levite your brother? I know that he can speak well. And look, he is also coming out to meet you. When he sees you, he will be glad in his heart. Now you shall speak to him and put the words in his mouth. And I will be with your mouth and with his mouth, and I will teach you what you shall do (Ex. 4:10–15, NKJV).

(1) Was Moses' objection to God's plan for him a valid protest?

_____

_____

(2) Why do you think he raised it?

_____

_____

_____

(3) The Bible tells us that God was angered by Moses' response (and not for the last time, either). So, why did God persevere? Why didn't He just choose somebody else?

_____

_____

_____

(4) Was Moses' ability to discern what was really "right" for him very well developed at this point in his life?

_____

_____

_____

(5) Based on what you may already know about Moses and his long-term leadership of the Children of Israel, would you say that his ability to discern what was best for him, the will of God, and what was best for his people developed in a positive way over the course of his lifetime? Explain your reasoning.

_____

_____

_____

(6) What does the example of Moses' discernment suggest about your own situation?

_____

_____

_____

_____

> ## FOR DEEPER CONSIDERATION . . . WHAT ABOUT HITLER?
>
> *Consider the millions of people who failed to discern what Adolph Hitler was up to during the holocaust, among his own countrymen but also among other people from around the world. Some people saw the evidence and deduced what was going on, and many people claimed after all the evidence was in that they had known all along (thus alleging discernment), but few people in the public eye actually called the evil of Adolph Hitler what it was on the public record. This is really the only measure we can go by more than 60 years later. Had the world really known, would not the public outcry have been far greater than it was?*

THE SOURCE OF TRUE DISCERNMENT

I don't believe it's possible for men and women to discern the difference between good and evil entirely on their own. If it were possible, I still wouldn't recommend that approach! I believe that the best discernment, the kind we need so we can follow the good and avoid the evil *when the differences are the most difficult to determine*, comes only from God.

WORDS TO REMEMBER . . .

For everyone who partakes only of milk is unskilled in the word of righteousness, for he is a babe. But solid food belongs to those who are of full age, that is, those who by reason of use have their senses exercised to discern both good and evil (Heb. 5:13–15, NKJV).

CLOSING PRAYER . . .

—◊◊◊—

Our Father, increase the wisdom of our minds to develop our powers of deduction and give to us the wisdom of the Holy Spirit to develop our powers of discernment.

May we not fall victim to Satan's wiles; may we know what he's about and trust You and You alone to help us avoid his traps. In Jesus' name, Amen.

6

―⁓―

EXTINGUISHING FIERY DARTS

When Paul spoke of the "shield of faith with which you will be able to quench all the fiery darts of the wicked one" (Eph. 6:16, NKJV), he was using language perfectly suited to his time and place. Everyone knew that a "fiery dart" was a flaming arrow, for even those who hadn't been in battle against Roman soldiers knew about their weaponry.

What terminology might Paul use today to adapt his illustration for a modern audience? Grenade? Cluster bomb? Or, during the Civil War era, perhaps "grapeshot"?

In truth it's not the terminology that counts; it's the concept. Here, the concept is of a destructive device that lets a single shot (or "toss," or "drop") do far-reaching damage. To put it another way, the devil uses something the financial experts call "leverage"—*letting a little bit of effort do a lot of work.*

As we have seen repeatedly, this is what the devil does best. He seldom tells a huge lie, and he seldom fires a big bullet. Instead, he lets our own "human nature" work against us to magnify the effect of his most feeble-seeming efforts. Except, of course, that they are never really "feeble" at all—they are much more like viruses that sneak inside in the dark and stay hidden until they're big and strong enough to destroy their host.

That's us—but let us not be innocent hosts any longer!

SATAN LOVES CERTAIN ATTITUDES!

The list below, on the left side, contains a dozen common emotions, or attitudes, that Satan often uses against us. To see some examples of how Satan used each of these in biblical times, match up the items in the list with the passages on the right that best illustrate each one.

Anger	(1) Genesis 37:3, 4
Pride	(2) Jeremiah 15:17
Discouragement	(3) Matthew 27:4, 5
Doubt	(4) Genesis 4:8
Fear	(5) John 6:17–19
Loneliness	(6) Matthew 23:5–7
Rejection	(7) Numbers 14:1–4
Jealousy	(8) Judges 16:1
Guilt	(9) Genesis 38:6–26
Unforgiveness	(10) John 20:27
Lust	(11) Matthew 12:7, 8
Greed	(12) Matthew 14:30

Without God's help we can all fall victim to any of these, at any time.

STRAIGHT FROM THE BOOK . . .

It is in our minds that we remember, we understand, we make decisions, we fantasize, and we evaluate truth from fiction. It is with our minds that we believe, we acknowledge God, and we make choices. The battleground with Satan is the mind.

FOR HIS EYES ONLY . . .

Choose any of the emotions, or attitudes, in the preceding list—but preferably one that you've wrestled with more than the others. Make your own list of at least three times in your life when you've fallen victim to one of Satan's fiery darts promoting that attitude. Then write a personal note to God, thanking Him specifically (and in as much detail as you can) for rescuing you from that situation and setting you back on the path toward righteousness. If you still wrestle with that emotion, ask God to renew your strength and help you to recognize and resist any additional darts that the devil might send your way.

HOW DOES THE DEVIL DO HIS WORK?

Every Sunday school student knows the story of Judas, who betrayed our Savior to the Romans on behalf of the chief priests. He was then so distressed by what he had done that he tried to give the money back. Eventually he hanged himself.

However, as familiar as the story may be, there is an important point to be made with respect to Judas that isn't always discussed. First, Turn to Luke 22:1–6 and read these six verses.

Now the Feast of Unleavened Bread drew near, which is called _____. And the chief priests and the scribes sought how they might kill Him, for they _____ the people.

Then Satan entered Judas, surnamed Iscariot, who was numbered among the twelve. So he went his way and conferred with the chief priests and captains, how he might betray Him to them. And they were glad, and agreed to give him _____. So he promised and sought opportunity to betray Him to them in the absence of the multitude (NKJV).

☞Now turn to John 13, read verse 2, and then verse 27. Consider the questions that follow.

And supper being ended, the devil having already put it into the heart of Judas Iscariot, Simon's son, to _____ Him . . . (NKJV).

Now after the piece of bread, Satan _____ him. Then Jesus said to him, "What you do, do quickly" (NKJV).

(1) What do these Scriptures tell us about Satan's "working methods"? In Judas' case, did he do all his work at once, or did he possibly do it over a period of time?

_____

_____

_____

(2) Expand on your answer to the question above. What is the overall pattern you see in these verses? When do you think Satan first approached Judas about betraying Jesus? Do you think the decision to betray Jesus was settled in Judas' mind before the Passover Supper or not?

_____

_____

(3) Most important, what is the personal lesson you believe
God would like you to take with you from this discussion?

_____

_____

_____

FOR DEEPER CONSIDERATION . . .

*Connect this discussion about Judas with what we talked about in chapter
5, on discernment. By which method did Christ know that Judas was about
to betray Him—deduction or discernment?*

_____

_____

_____

*At the same time, did the other eleven disciples know what was going on
"behind the scenes"?*

_____

_____

_____

What was the evidence, one way or the other?

_____

_____

_____

*If the other disciples failed to discern Judas' intent, why do you think your
conclusion might be true?*

_____

_____

_____

STRAIGHT FROM THE BOOK . . .

Toehold —*The more you entertain a thought aimed at a need you feel, the more that thought looms in your mind until it crowds out all other thoughts.*

Foothold—*If you entertain thoughts repeatedly—over days, weeks, or months—the thoughts take root in you and become normal to you.*

Stronghold—*Habitual patterns of thinking become strongholds in our minds.*

AN IMPORTANT DISTINCTION

Turn to Genesis 11:1–9, and fill in the blanks:

Now the whole earth had one language and one speech. And it came to pass, as they journeyed from the east, that they found a plain in the land of Shinar, and they _____ there. Then they said to one another, "Come, let us make bricks and bake them thoroughly." They had brick for stone, and they had asphalt for mortar.

And they said, "Come, let us build ourselves a _____, and a _____ whose top is in the heavens; let us make a name for ourselves, lest we be scattered abroad over the face of the whole earth."

But the LORD came down to see the city and the tower which the sons of men had built. And the LORD said, "Indeed the people are one and they all have one language, and this is what they begin to do; now nothing that they propose to do will be _____ from them. Come, let Us go down and there confuse their language, that they may not understand one another's speech." So the LORD _____ them abroad from there over the face of all the earth, and they ceased building the city. Therefore its name is called Babel, because there the LORD _____ the language of all the earth; and from there the LORD scattered them abroad over the face of all the earth (NKJV).

↠This story may also be familiar to you, but please look at it in a fresh way through answering the following questions:

(1) Was (and is) there anything inherently wrong with building a city or a tower?

_____

_____

_____

(2) Assuming you answered "no," what, then, was wrong with what the people in the land of Shinar were trying to do? Was there a sin involved, and if so, what was it?

_____

_____

_____

Could we, in the modern age, also be guilty of the same sin?

_____

_____

_____

If so, why does God not punish us as He did the people in the land of Shinar?

_____

_____

_____

_____

HOW DOES THE DEVIL GAIN ACCESS
TO OUR HEARTS AND MINDS?

Nothing in the Bible (or in mankind's experience since biblical times) suggests that there is anything wrong with using bricks and mortar to build houses and other functional buildings for ourselves. Surely we should also be encouraged to make them as beautiful as we can, even as the Lord has created such a beautiful world for us to put them in!

However, Satan is obviously capable of turning even an *honorable* activity into something that *dis*honors God. In this way he gains control of our hearts and minds: first he selects *good* abilities, activities, and interests, and second he sends those fiery darts that trick and seduce us into perverting to evil what started out to be good.

> ### STRAIGHT FROM THE BOOK . . .
>
> *In the natural, the flaming arrows to which Paul referred were arrows common to Roman battles. . . . In the spiritual, flaming arrows refer to the bombardment of the mind with thoughts, impressions, and impulses that are contrary to God's purposes. These thoughts might be thoughts to do evil. They might be angry thoughts, sinful thoughts, or temptations to sin.*

In each of the following passages from the Bible, someone was engaged in something positive that Satan turned into something negative. Read the passage, identify the person (or people) involved, name the activity he or she was pursuing that would be honorable or positive under normal circumstances, and identify what Satan turned it into. Then indicate what method Satan used. The first one is finished for you.

(Note that the person doing the positive activity does NOT have to be the person deriving the negative result.)

Scripture	Person	Positive Activity	Negative Result	Satan's Method
(1) Genesis 3:1–7	Eve/ Adam	Eating	First Sin	Lies and insinuations
(2) 2 Kings 20:12, 13				▼

▼

(3) 1 Samuel 13:8–14

_____

(4) 1 Kings 16:20—1 Kings 21:25
(long, but fascinating!)

_____

(5) Matthew 2:1–8; 16, 17

_____

(6) Luke 6:6–10

_____

(7) Luke 5:29–32

_____

One more question related to the above: given the difference between a toehold, a foothold, and a stronghold (see "Straight from the Book—A Composite Quote," page 76), in the table you just completed, which of those three general classifications would each of the listings fall into? Each entry in the table is numbered; write your answers in the corresponding spaces below, as in example #1. Also note that the entire story of any entry could fall into all three categories.

(1) Toehold and foothold

(2) _____

(3) _____

(4) _____

(5) _____

(6) _____

(7) _____

STRAIGHT FROM THE BOOK . . .

If Satan is capable of deceiving you, craftily manipulating you, and seducing you to yield to temptation in one area of your life, he's going to come back again and again to that area.

A VERY PERSONAL EXERCISE!

The table (or "grid") below can be used to help you apply what you know about Satan and his methods and to do some deeper thinking. The goal is to look at each item, or activity, as objectively as possible but without abandoning anything the Lord has already taught you. The grid should be used to stimulate your thoughts and, if you are in a group setting with like-minded people, to enhance your thinking in the company of others.

However, be aware that many of the topics, while somewhat "generalized," can lead very quickly to rather heated discussions even among practicing Christians! So, I urge you to pursue this exercise privately, on your own, before you discuss it with others. In the "activity" column I also urge you to add categories that are more specific to your own life.

Overall, the goal is to see as graphically as possible how Satan is able to "shoot his fiery darts" at us even when we are engaged in worthwhile pursuits that could honor God, and thereby turn them against God.

Activity	Example—Honors God	Example—Dishonors God
Art (Painting)	Ceiling of Sistine Chapel	Paintings of animal waste products
Music		
Architecture		
Sculpture		
Literature		
Philosophy		
Education		
Politics		

Don't Miss the CMD

CMD stands for "Critical Moment of Decision." Every sin we commit—small or large, once or many times, comes with its own moment of decision. Those CMDs pile up on one side or the other of the ledger, even as the decisions they represent get easier and easier to make—for good or bad.

I remember a story an older gentlemen once told me about his son. Danny had been a church kid most of his life: saved as a teenager, president of his youth group, and student at a well-known Bible college, although he never got the teaching degree he said he wanted. Instead, he got married

> **Straight from the Book . . .**
>
> *Temptations, doubts, accusations, justifications, and speculations begin in the mind. Our feet, hands, and bodies follow where the mind leads us.*

in his junior year and then needed money, so he took a factory job, then drifted for several years, and eventually dropped out of fellowship with other believers altogether.

Years later he came back to the church and the faith of his youth, but not without many hair-raising adventures along the way. Some of his experiences, involving armed robberies and other big-city crimes that he was victimized by, could have taken his life. As he readily admitted, most were brought on entirely by his own desire to do things "on his own" with no interference from God.

His father once asked him if he could identify the moment he first began to slip off the path. To the older man's surprise, Danny knew instantly what he was talking about.

"I know this sounds crazy, but one time I went to the grocery store, gave them the only ten-dollar bill I had, and discovered when I got home that I still had ten dollars, plus change for what I'd given the clerk. I knew instantly that she thought I'd given her a twenty, and I simply hadn't been paying attention. I argued with myself for one whole evening about whether I should go back down there and tell them what had happened, but in the end I didn't do it.

"That one event became like the first leak in the dike for me. Every time I went into that store from that day on I felt guilty, but instead of trying to make it right I began to see it as a game and tried to find other ways to "get ahead" by cheating. I never got caught, but even as I became a small-time cheat I became a big-time liar to myself, and to God. From that little start eventually I fell completely out of fellowship. I couldn't stand to be around the church anymore, because I knew I was living a lie. It was too easy to keep going in the other direction once I got started."

Eventually I got a chance to talk to Danny myself and asked him to clarify one thing. What was it in his life, in his witness, in his makeup, that let him go sideways and do something so "uncharacteristic" of the Danny we'd all known as a youth? Without hesitation he responded.

"I knew I had the power to do the right, but to do that I had to out-argue something that almost seemed like an audible voice in my ear. It told me that I needed the money and I should keep it—that I'd be a fool to take it back. I lost the argument."

⤇ For His Eyes Only . . . ⤆

A surprising number of people—many of them long-term believers and solid Christians—can tell stories a lot like Danny's. I feel very sad to say this, but I think there are many more out there who could tell similar stories, too, except that theirs do not have happy endings.

If you have such a story in your background, but if you've finally put all the sideways walking behind you, write a note to God detailing what happened, to the best of your recollection. Then thank Him, profusely, for helping you find your way back into fellowship with Him!

On the other hand, if you haven't yet come back into your former relationship with God, ask Him right now to accept your repentance and forgive you for whatever you've done. He'll do it; all it takes is a willingness to confess and a determination to make a 180-degree turn and go forward, from that point on, in His strength.

WORDS TO REMEMBER . . .

Enter by the narrow gate; for wide is the gate and broad is the way that leads to destruction, and there are many who go in by it (Matt. 7:13, NKJV).

CLOSING PRAYER . . .

Our Father, we thank You and praise Your name anew for giving us the faith to depend entirely on You—to trust You alone, Father, to keep our footsteps centered on the path of righteousness. We know that we cannot be faithful to You on our own—all that we are comes from You, including our very thoughts. May these continue to be centered on You, and may our determination to keep You and Your truth as the focus of our lives never waver.

In Jesus' name, Amen.

7

—◦◦—

THE STRATEGY UNDERLYING
EVERY TEMPTATION

Given all the military conflicts around the globe in recent years, much has been made of the difference between strategy and tactics. If you're an out-of-office politician, wanting to attack whoever is in charge at the moment, you can criticize his *overall plan or* the *way he's doing things at the moment.*

The first is a strategy; the second is a tactic.

To bring this down to a personal level, if you decide to become a lawyer by (1) earning the best grades you can get in school, (2) clerking at the courthouse during the summers, (3) joining every debate club you can find, (4) competing for scholarships to the best universities and law schools, and (5) learning to laugh at jokes you hate, you've settled on a *strategy*.

Numbers (1) through (4) are all *tactics*, meaning the individual things you do—the methods you use—to put your plan into action. Remember all this the next time you hear some football coach called a "great tactician." Many people confuse the terms and get *plans* confused with *methods*.

Military commanders, football and basketball coaches, and those who do the best job of raising healthy, wholesome kids, both mothers *and* fathers, all deal in both strategies and tactics.

THE DEVIL DOES THE SAME THING

The devil has a strategy, too. In fact, he has more than one. For you he has a *personal* strategy. His goal is to wreck your life and destroy your eternal relationship with God with a plan tailored to you and your situation.

With respect to the God who made all things, Satan has what he thinks of as a *master* strategy. Satan might call it *cosmic*, but that name would give him too much credit! Nonetheless, the goal of his master strategy is to ruin God's plan of salvation for all eternity. He still wants to replace God with himself, even though he is already defeated.

Satan uses personal strategies to undermine *us*. To him that's also another way of undermining God. Just think of the lies Satan must have told Lamech (Gen. 4:23, 24) to get him to kill a young boy for merely bumping into him. This action would have compromised any righteous relationship with God that Lamech might have had up to that point.

Then think of the lies Satan told Christ Himself during His forty days in the wilderness, hoping to ruin God's perfect plan of salvation all in one triumphant move. It is the same dynamic in both cases— just on a grander scale when he tempted our Savior.

One additional fact about Satan is that he is not really very creative. In John 8:44, several translations of the Bible (e.g., NIV, AMP, NLT, and ESV) call him the "father of lies," for he relies on falsehoods, repeated over and over with only minor variations. Thus, his personal strategies for each of us tend to involve three basic, oft-repeated strategic moves, or *tactics*.

(1) Strategic Move #1: He focuses on our needs and convinces us that we have to fulfill them—now!

(2) Strategic Move #2: He convinces us to use an ungodly means to gain a godly end.

(3) Strategic Move #3: He convinces us to take advantage of an urgent opportunity that won't be good for us in the long run.

Satan sometimes uses *all three* of the above. For example, the story of the temptation of Adam and Eve (Gen. 3:1–6) has often been used as a classic illustration of how Satan used all three tactics. *First*, he convinced Eve that he had a great way to fulfill a normal need, her hunger. *Second*, he convinced her that what God had forbidden wasn't really ungodly at all, but instead would bring her to a godly end. *Third*, he convinced her that he was offering her an instant transformation, and thus she needed to *do it now*.

Let's look at another clear example, involving the Children of Israel in the wilderness, at Mt. Sinai. Look up Exodus 32:1–6, fill in the blanks, and then answer the questions that follow.

Now when the people saw that Moses _____ coming down from the mountain, the people gathered together to Aaron, and said to him, "Come, _____ us gods that shall go before us; for as for this Moses, the man who brought us up out of the land of Egypt, we do not know what has become of him."

And Aaron said to them, "_____ _____ the golden earrings which are in the ears of your wives, your sons, and your daughters, and bring them to me." So all the people broke off the golden earrings which were in their ears, and brought them to Aaron. And he received the gold from their hand, and he _____ it with an engraving tool, and made a molded calf.

Then they said, "This is your god, O Israel, that brought you out of the land of Egypt!"

So when Aaron saw it, he built an altar before it. And Aaron made a proclamation and said, "Tomorrow is a feast to the LORD." Then they rose early on the next day, offered burnt offerings, and _____ peace offerings; and the people sat down to eat and drink, and rose up to play (NKJV).

Isn't it almost impossible to read this passage without seeing the influence of Satan at work? No question about it—he manipulated the

Children of Israel using the masterful skills he has. So, rather than asking *who* he influenced and *when* he did it, let's talk about *how* and *what*.

(1) What needs did Satan identify in the Children of Israel?

_____

_____

_____

(2) What might he have said to them about fulfilling those needs?

_____

_____

_____

(3) What was the godly end he probably told them they had a right to pursue?

_____

_____

_____

(4) What were the ungodly means he convinced them to use to pursue it?

_____

_____

_____

(5) How did Satan introduce and develop the concept of an urgent opportunity? That is, how did he convince the people that they had to do something right now?

_____

_____

_____

FOR DEEPER CONSIDERATION . . .

Do the satanic methods we've discussed and illustrated here serve as a reminder for you? What modern industry has studied, tested, and refined the same methods, over and over again, until the best practitioners are able to manipulate vast segments of the general population at any given time on any given subject? And I don't mean the mainstream media, either, although a case might be made for them as well!

I'm talking about advertising, the industry that convinces all of us, in subtle and not-so-subtle ways, to buy various products. The only satanic method they don't necessarily use is #2 (using ungodly means to gain a godly end). On the other hand, we could expand the definition of "ungodly" to include anything that works against the best interests of one of God's creations, meaning people just like me and you! For example, when ghetto teenagers, whose families can barely afford food, insist on wearing $200 sneakers because that's the "cool" thing to do . . . well, what about it? Have some modern business practices gone too far? What can we do to restore the proper balance in our own and our children's lives? Write your thoughts here:

_____

_____

_____

_____

_____

A FEW MORE EXAMPLES

Look up and read the Scriptures in column one of the following table. Then list the person against whom Satan used one (or even *all*) of the three tactics we've already discussed. (For your convenience they are listed again at the bottom of the table.) Then put an "X" in the correct column (or columns) to indicate which tactics Satan used, based either on what the Bible tells us he *said or did* or on what the person's actions *suggest* that Satan did. The first entry is worked for you.

(Note: Not all of these stories are familiar, and even the *familiar* ones aren't necessarily obvious. Also, the length of most of these scripture references is minimized in the table; almost all could be expanded to include more context surrounding the basic story. I urge you to read *more* than the minimum, in each case, for deeper understanding of each situation.)

Scripture	Person	#1	#2	#3	Did it work?
(Sample) Genesis 3:1–6	Eve/Adam	X		X	Yes
(1) Numbers 12:1–15					
(2) Any or *all* of the Book of Job					
(3) 1 Kings 16:8–20					
(4) Esther 3:1— end of book					
(5) Judges 16:4–20					
(6) 2 Samuel 11:1–4					
(7) Numbers 22:2–6					
(8) Acts 7:58; 8:1–3					
(9) Luke 10:38–42					
(10) Acts 15:36–40					

(1) Strategic Move #1: He focuses on our *needs* and convinces us that we *have to fulfill them* now!

(2) Strategic Move #2: He convinces us to use an ungodly means to gain a godly end.

(3) Strategic Move #3: He convinces us to take advantage of an *urgent opportunity*.

After you have finished the table, add up all the checkmarks and divide by the number of tactical situations involved (which should be 10). This exercise will give you an "Average Tactics per Situation" (ATS) number.

Write it here: _____

≈►What does that number tell you about Satan's tactics—does he tend to use *several* or just *one* of them?

_____

_____

_____

≈►What, then, can you expect him to use against *you*?

_____

_____

_____

IN GROUP SETTINGS . . .

Create your own ATS table, based on the Scriptures you are already familiar with. Challenge other members of your group to fill out the table you create. See who can create the longest table within 20 minutes, with Scripture references included. Then see who can provide the best answers within a specified time limit.

REMEMBER—SATAN NEVER SURRENDERS!

The second major thing to remember about Satan, in addition to recognizing his methods, is that he does not give up just because you resisted him once. Or twice, or three times, or even many more times.

In a sense, modern terrorists who kill innocent people out of pure malice are modeling Satan's techniques. This should not be a surprise, for Satan is the evil spirit they serve. Like him, they are *relentless* and often refuse to surrender, or they pretend to surrender only to spring back into action the minute you lower your guard.

Remember—deceiving, sabotaging, and

STRAIGHT FROM THE BOOK . . .

A temptation is an enticement by the devil that always includes sin and is always aimed at destroying us in some way. A temptation can occur through the devil speaking directly to our minds and hearts, or by the devil speaking through a human being who is functioning under the devil's influence.

subverting make up Satan's *entire job description*, his "life's work." He simply does not surrender. If he cannot fool you on Tuesday, maybe your guard will be down on Saturday night.

STRAIGHT FROM THE BOOK . . .

Can God meet your emotional needs? Absolutely. But it is on this point that people are most often tripped up. They don't trust God for love and acceptance. They don't believe God will help them discover their gifts and become competent in using them. They don't feel worthy—perhaps because they have been told repeatedly that they are unworthy or because they feel that their sins put them beyond the realm of worthiness in God's eyes.

The Bible contains many stories of people who gave in to Satan's temptations—some right away, some after long temptations. Several of these stories are listed below. Many you will not even need to look up, but just in case, the references are included.

In the answer space, indicate whether the person in question surrendered to Satan after being tempted once, twice, or multiple times. If the text doesn't make the answer clear, give your best guess from the context.

(1) Jonah and his refusal to go to Nineveh (all of Jonah)

_____

(2) Reuben and his father's concubine (Gen. 35:22)

_____

(3) Abimelech and the murder of his half-brothers (Judg. 9:5)

_____

(4) Jezebel and the murder of Naboth (1 Kin. 21:7–14)

_____

(5) Amnon and the rape of Tamar (2 Sam. 13:10–14)

_____

(6) Joash, commanding Zechariah to be stoned (2 Chr. 10–18)

_____

(7) Joseph's brothers and the sale of Joseph (Gen. 37:28–33)

_____

(8) Judas and his betrayal of Christ (Matt. 26:14–25)

_____

(9) Potiphar's wife and her lie about Joseph (Gen. 39:7–12)

_____

PERSONAL APPLICATION

Now let's bring the previous exercise into the modern age—perhaps even into our own lives or those of people we know. Read the following list of "situations" and offer suggestions for those who might find themselves in any of them. What might people do to avoid being victimized by Satan's repeated overtures?

A person who . . .

(1) has a love for gossip, fights against it, but is asked to join an intercessory prayer group . . .

_____

(2) travels a lot, stays in hotels with TVs/VCRs, and has a problem with pornography . . .

_____

(3) loves jewelry, gets a job in a jewelry store, and is often alone with the inventory . . .

_____

(4) knows that the neighbor's wife fancies him and is invited over to fix a faucet while her husband is away . . .

_____

(5) administers construction contracts for an entire state and frequently receives free gifts by mail from various contractors . . .

_____

(6) realizes that a teacher has made a huge mistake in his favor in grading a test . . .

_____

☞If you are in a group setting, can you think of additional situations for the group to consider?

_____

_____

_____

_____

NEVER LOSE SIGHT OF SATAN'S ULTIMATE GOALS . . .

❑   To draw you away from God
❑   To thwart's God's purpose for your life
❑   To deny the glory of God in your life
❑   To destroy you in any way he can, including any physical harm he can bring

All for the purpose of harming God's perfect plans for ALL of mankind! Repeat after me:

With God's help, I will not be Satan's pawn!

WORDS TO REMEMBER . . .

Finally, my brethren, be strong in the Lord and in the power of His might. Put on the whole armor of God, that you may be able to stand against the wiles of the devil. For we do not wrestle against flesh and blood, but against principalities, against powers, against the rulers of the darkness of this age, against spiritual hosts of wickedness in the heavenly places (Eph. 6:10–12, NKJV).

CLOSING PRAYER . . .

Our Father, help me to be watchful against the lies and treacheries of Satan. Help me to recognize his tactics and fight against his strategies by relying on You, in everything I do, every moment of every day.

In Jesus' name, Amen.

STRAIGHT FROM THE BOOK . . .

The devil comes to you at a time of neediness—emotional, physical, spiritual—but his temptation is aimed at one of your strengths.

8

RESPONDING TO TEMPTATION

I have a friend who was reared in a large family with nine brothers and sisters. He and his siblings are now in their 40s and 50s, but every time they gather together for holidays they still amuse themselves with tales of their childhood.

There is nothing new in this, except that over the years they have gradually developed an annual competition to identify that year's *"Greatest Excuse Anyone Ever Invented."* The goal is to recall actual, *real-life attempts* to fool their parents and "get away' with something. So far, the Grand Prize Winner of All Time is the story of the brother who crawled into the attic, planning to make scary noises above his sisters' bedroom late at night.

Unfortunately, after waiting for hours for his big chance, he finally began his ghostly serenade only to be frightened in the total darkness by what was probably a small nesting squirrel that ran across his face. He thrashed so hard he slipped off the beam he was resting on and crashed through the ceiling, onto one of the beds.

His excuse? He'd been up there looking for a long-lost Waterford crystal bowl his grandparents had once owned, which they'd brought themselves from Ireland. His "plan," if he should find it, was to polish it, wrap it, and present it triumphantly to his parents as a Christmas present.

His parents were not fooled. To be sure, *no* one who has ever reared a child will have trouble recognizing the word *excuses*—the more inventive the better! Our childhood experiences with inventing excuses—with finding some plausible way to duck responsibility for our actions—does not end, for many people, with childhood.

STRAIGHT FROM THE BOOK . . .

Many people waver when it comes to resisting temptations. They aren't quite sure they want to resist temptations—at least not all temptations, all the time, and in all circumstances. Many people want to be able to pick and choose the sin they fall into, generally because they think they can quickly erase any damage caused by that sin.

GOD IS NOT FOOLED

Not my own experience or that of hundreds of other ministers and counselors equals the first and final word of the Lord Himself. Thousands of years ago, the God Who created us and knows all things was aware of what we often do, when confronted with situations in which the only *honest* approach would be to take responsibility for our own mistakes.

≪≫Look up the following passages in the Bible and fill in the blanks. Then answer the questions that follow.

Ecclesiastes 5:6
Do not let your mouth cause your flesh to sin, nor say before the messenger of God that it was an error. Why should God be angry at your _____ and destroy the work of your hands? (NKJV)

Some translations insert the word "made" before the word "angry" in the second sentence of this verse, to clarify the meaning. Either way, it contains a typical Hebrew "turn of phrase" (see the "Why So Many Questions" section) that uses a question rather than a simple statement to make its point more emphatic.

WHY SO MANY QUESTIONS?

The "question format" is what we might call an idiomatic technique in ancient Hebrew, preserved even today in the Jewish culture by a certain tendency to put a real "point" on questions. For example, rather than saying "Why didn't you call me?" someone might say, "So . . . your fingers were all broken and you couldn't dial the phone?" The latter is both more colorful and more difficult to ignore. It also tends to convey a sense of urgency, almost to obligate the listener to respond right away.

---

(1) Why, indeed, should you be so foolish as to make God angry by trying to fool Him with false excuses? Which do you think would be more likely to make God angry— your sin or your excuse?

_____

_____

_____

(2) Why would that be true, and on what do you base your answer?

_____

_____

_____

John 15:22

If I had not come and spoken to them, they would have no sin, but now they have no _____ for their sin (NKJV).

Romans 1:20

For since the creation of the world His invisible attributes are clearly seen, being understood by the things that are made,

even His eternal power and Godhead, so that they are without _____ (NKJV).

Some people have read the two verses above as an excuse to do
exactly the opposite of what Christ commanded us to do in the Great
Commission (Matt. 28:19; Mark 16:15). That is, to *not* engage in
evangelism because *with understanding comes responsibility.*

❧Why, therefore, should we "gift" others with a responsibility they
would not have if we'd left them alone? Do you believe this is a
wrong interpretation? Why?

_____

_____

_____

_____

_____

_____

THE ULTIMATE NON-EXCUSE . . .

*Many people down through history and even today have tried to take a
"top-of-the-fence" position to the effect that Jesus Christ might have been a
great man, a great teacher, and perhaps even a great prophet chosen by God,
but was not God Himself.*

*However, in the classic book called Mere Christianity, well-known
author C.S. Lewis argued that Christ left us with no such middle-of-the-
road position at all—entirely on purpose! Given the extreme nature of
what Christ Himself claimed to be, said Lewis, Christ was either insane or
he was telling the truth and was, indeed, God. There is no middle ground.
If he were insane, it would be even greater insanity on our part to call him
a great teacher, prophet, or anything else of that nature! Therefore, there is
really only one rational position left—the very one God referred to when he
said "they are without excuse."*

*Christ is God, and we are, indeed, without excuse if we fail to recog-
nize Him as such.*

STRIPPING AWAY ALL EXCUSES

Even though we never seem to run out of variations, when all is said and done, most people who try to avoid personal responsibility for committing sins use one of five basic excuses. All five excuses are listed directly below. After each one there is a blank line suitable for writing the number of the logical match up, or "corollary," for each excuse. Excuses are conveniently listed below the five false justifications. Demonstrate that you understand the differences between the five excuses by matching them with their logical corollaries.

EXCUSES

Excuse #1: Somebody else made me do it.

_____

Excuse #2: God made me do it.

_____

Excuse #3: God knows I'm weak.

_____

Excuse #4: This is different.

_____

Excuse #5: I've thought about it so I might as well do it.

_____

COROLLARIES

(C) . . . so obviously it's not my fault.

(A) . . . because no one else has ever been in this position before.

(B) . . . and therefore shouldn't have given me so much to handle!

(E) . . . so obviously it's His fault!

(D) . . . since it's already a done deal in my heart.

STRAIGHT FROM THE BOOK . . .

Those with a wavering commitment to Jesus as Lord repeatedly give in to temptations because they don't have a firm resolve not to sin.

IT ALL BEGAN WITH THAT APPLE

Genesis 3:12, 13 tells us:

> Then the man said, "The woman whom You gave to be with me, she gave me of the tree, and I ate."
> And the LORD God said to the woman, "What is this you have done?"
> The woman said, "The serpent deceived me, and I ate" (NKJV).

Clearly, both Adam and Eve offered basically the same false justification when God confronted them with the first sin in history. In other words, they chose excuse #1. Now go to the following table, which lists five different Scriptures. Look up and read each one. Then indicate who the main character(s) is (are) in each case, and list what sin was committed. Or, *note how they failed to respond positively to God's urging*, which is not always a sin but can be equally tragic. Finally, list the excuse(s) they *might* have used when they were found out, *whether or not the Scriptures tell us they actually used that excuse*. Be careful to use each of the five excuses at least one time each, even if you assign some of them more than once. Then answer the questions that follow.

Scripture	Main Character(s)	Sin or Failure	Excuse(s)
(1) Gen. 32:22–24			
(2) Matt. 19:20–22			
(3) 1 Sam. 13:8–14			
(4) 2 Sam. 11:2–5			
(5) Luke 10:38–42			

More about Satan's Methods

In everything the devil does to deceive us—including what we've already learned about supplying us with excuses—he also follows a clear pattern in how he presents his temptations.

❑ **First,** he presents what *seems reasonable.*

❑ **Second,** he suggests *questionable methods.*

❑ **Third,** he usually presents an *urgent timetable*—some reason to do it *now.*

✍ Turn to the Book of Jonah and reread as much as you need to refresh your memory of what happened when God called Jonah to go to Nineveh. Then, in the spaces below, apply what you know about the story to identify what Satan did in Jonah's own heart and mind to make Jonah do what seemed *reasonable* and *urgent,* using *questionable methods.* Also, what did Jonah do in *direct response* to the devil's attempts in each of the three categories?

(1) Reasonable:

_____

_____

_____

(2) Questionable:

_____

_____

_____

(3) Urgent:

_____

_____

_____

✑Now read Genesis 38:6–26 and respond to the same questions you answered above. However, concentrate on the actions of Tamar and not the actions of Judah in this selection. Even though Tamar's actions are not presented as "sins" in the Bible, Satan used the trickery of enticement. Indeed, as Judah said, in many ways she was more righteous than he was. Nonetheless, even though what Tamar was pursuing would have been an honorable goal in the Hebrew culture of that time and place, consider how Satan tricked her into attaining it.

(1) Reasonable:

_____

_____

_____

(2) Questionable:

_____

_____

_____

(3) Urgent:

_____

_____

_____

HOW DO YOU FEEL ABOUT THE JUDAH/TAMAR STORY?

The story of Tamar's trickery, by which she fooled her father-in-law and secured for herself a male child (indeed, she got twin boys!) can be confusing to modern readers. With respect to Tamar and Judah, who was the sinner here and who was the innocent party? Were they both sinners? Were they both innocent?

The Bible does not make clear distinctions within the story itself, but it does assume that the reader will already know something of ancient ▼

▼

Hebrew laws and customs. Here, Tamar was invoking one aspect of the Kinsman Redeemer customs, by which a childless widow had the right to expect her dead husband's brother to marry her and give her a male heir, to take care of her in her old age.

In addition, some things can be determined by what happened later. When it came time for Jacob to pass on the patriarchal blessing to his sons before his death, this is what he said of Judah, (Gen. 49:9–12):

> Judah is a lion's whelp;
>> From the prey, my son, you have gone up.
>> He bows down, he lies down as a lion;
>> And as a lion, who shall rouse him?
>> The scepter shall not depart from Judah,
>> Nor a lawgiver from between his feet,
>> Until Shiloh comes;
>> And to Him shall be the obedience of the people.
>> Binding his donkey to the vine,
>> And his donkey's colt to the choice vine,
>> He washed his garments in wine,
>> And his clothes in the blood of grapes.
>> His eyes are darker than wine,
>> And his teeth whiter than milk (NKJV).

As for Tamar, we find no specific condemnation within Scripture. Indeed, we know that a woman without a son was a second-class citizen in that era. Except for pure charity from someone who was under no legal obligation to care for her, without a son a Hebrew woman would be doomed to fend for herself in her old age (remember Ruth and Naomi), a frightening proposition—hence the common practice of requiring a man to marry his brother's wife and give her sons to care for her, if her own husband died prematurely.

Given all that, how would you now answer the "sin" and "guilt" questions from the end of the first paragraph above?

HOW DID JESUS RESPOND TO TEMPTATION?

The fourth chapter of Matthew answers this question, in brilliant detail. Each time the devil offered one of his lies, Jesus responded by quoting the truth from Scripture. He also did so immediately, and within a very short time, he put plenty of distance between Himself and Satan.

In response to Satan's temptations our pattern should be:

(1) **First**, respond with the truth—from Scripture, if you are able.
(2) **Second**, do it right now, before Satan has a chance to gain a foothold in your life.
(3) **Third**, tell Satan to leave . . . and then walk away from him *mentally, emotionally,* and *spiritually,* even if you can't leave him behind in a strictly *physical* sense!

"REASONABLE" AND "URGENT"

Satan's methods and the keywords that relate to false concepts #1 and #3 that he tries to promote include the concepts of "reasonable" and "urgent." The word *reasonable* occurs only once in the *New King James Version* Bible translation. In Romans 12:1 Paul says,

> I beseech you therefore, brethren, by the mercies of God, that you present your bodies a living sacrifice, holy, acceptable to God, which is your reasonable service (NKJV).

Certainly it could be argued that the message of this well-known, well-loved verse is as far away from any Satan-inspired distortions of reasonable as it could get.

Likewise, the word "urgent" occurs five times in the same translation—twice in Daniel, with reference to the king's decree that eventually landed Daniel in the fiery furnace and twice more in subtitles to Psalms of David. And, of course, once in Titus 3:14: "And let our people also learn to maintain good works, to meet *urgent* needs, that they may not be unfruitful."

What is the point? Never is anything of God presented as urgent, with the exception of His offer of salvation. Accepting this has always been the must *urgent* thing any man or woman could ever do

All other exhortations to urgency come from Satan.

WORDS TO REMEMBER . . .

Every good gift and every perfect gift is from above, and comes down from the Father of lights, with whom there is no variation or shadow of turning. Of His own will He brought us forth by the word of truth, that we might be a kind of firstfruits of His creatures (James 1:17, 18, NKJV).

CLOSING PRAYER . . .

Our Father, we thank You for providing such clear examples of how to deal with Satan. We thank You that You are with us constantly, strengthening our resolve and concentrating our focus on resisting the wiles of the devil.

We thank You for the witness and example of Christ, but most of all for the gift of salvation You have given us through Him.

In Jesus' name, Amen.

STRAIGHT FROM THE BOOK . . .

Temptations are not temptations to do good or to display righteousness. By its very definition, a temptation is a desire instilled into the heart and mind of a person prompting him to do something that is not good. God will never tempt someone to sin.

9

—∿—

STAYING DRESSED FOR BATTLE

Every time I go into a large store—a warehouse store, a home improvement store, and even some of the smaller department stores—I seem to see the same thing. Many of the people who work in the backstage area, who do any lifting at all, are wearing wide belts, cinched up tight and extending above and sometimes even below the waist. This is a new development. Twenty or thirty years ago I don't think I ever saw such a thing.

The belts I'm talking about are made of reinforced nylon or some other strong but flexible material that will not "give" or stretch. It's my understanding that they protect the lower back when a person picks up something heavy, by adding extra support. Weightlifters often wear something similar, although their belts tend to be made of heavy leather.

Why? What gives? Why are people so determined to protect the mid-body?

IT'S NOT A NEW IDEA

Actually, wearing a protective belt around the middle is not a new idea at all. Ancient Roman soldiers wore heavy leather belts that, in some cases, were almost as wide as a woman's girdle from the mid-1900s.

Often they were reinforced with pieces of metal that might have looked like decorations, but which also had a much more practical purpose.

Roman soldiers were not so concerned with protecting the muscles of their lower backs They wore heavy belts to protect their vital organs from knives, swords, and arrows, not to mention heavy blows from various instruments. Any "decoration" that might help deflect a sharp point—well, so much the better—and they rarely took them off.

BELT-OF-TRUTH RELATIONSHIPS

Since most Sunday school attendees have heard much of what has been mentioned, let's consider what the items of battle-dress represent.

More than anything else the belt (-of-truth) was designed to protect vital organs, and the vital organs of Roman soldiers that were most vulnerable to life-threatening injury were those in the mid-body. These organs involved processing food, eliminating waste, and reproduction, which always involves relationships, since reproduction symbolizes long-term relationship, protecting this area of the body was vital for continuing the human race and therefore its connection with God.

In Paul's letter to the Ephesians, the Roman soldier's belt of protection becomes the *Belt of Truth* (Eph. 6:14). What a marvelous connection this is. Surely there can be no firmer foundation, for fighting off evil by building positive relationships with other people, than *Truth* with a capital T!

"Worthwhile things" that come from truth-based relationships include children, of course, through marriage. Worthwhile things that result from relationships with people other than a spouse also include physical, emotional, and spiritual support, both incoming and outgoing. They include the renewed strength and the increased capacity for service to God and others that develop through positive, personal interactions.

There's a reason men and women, with righteous hearts and minds, need other men and women of similar character: God made humans for godly relationship and interaction.

As iron sharpens iron, so a man sharpens the countenance of his friend (Prov. 27:17, NKJV).

❧Let's look at three of the most striking "sharpening-each-other" relationships in the Bible, each of which demonstrates how girding ourselves with Paul's *Belt of Truth* creates relationships that honor both God and ourselves. Read the following story from the life of David, taken from Second Samuel 9:1–7. Fill in the blanks and then answer the questions.

Now David said, "Is there still anyone who is left of the house of Saul, that I may show him _____ for Jonathan's sake?" And there was a servant of the house of Saul whose name was Ziba. So when they had called him to David, the king said to him, "Are you Ziba?" He said, "At your service!"

Then the king said, "Is there not still someone of the house of Saul [Ed. note: for the sake of Jonathan, Saul's son], to whom I may show the kindness of God?" And Ziba said to the king, "There is still a son of Jonathan who is _____ in his feet." So the king said to him, "Where is he?"

And Ziba said to the king, "Indeed he is in the house of Machir the son of Ammiel, in Lo Debar." Then King David sent and brought him out of the house of Machir the son of Ammiel, from Lo Debar.

Now when Mephibosheth the son of Jonathan, the son of Saul, had come to David, he fell on his face and prostrated himself. Then David said, "Mephibosheth?" And he answered, "Here is your servant!"

So David said to him, "Do not fear, for I will surely show you kindness for Jonathan your father's _____, and will restore to you all the land of Saul your grandfather; and you shall eat bread at my table continually."

This particular story almost brings tears to my eyes every time I read it. Can you imagine the terror Mephibosheth must have felt when David sent for him? And then the intense relief and joy!

After all, Mephibosheth—who was hiding out and living in near-poverty when David sought him out—was the grandson of the same King Saul who had done everything he could to kill David several years before. It was almost common custom for kings of the biblical era to solidify their power by killing all those who might someday become rivals for their throne. Saul was both jealous and terrified of David, but David had a wholly different attitude toward God's anointed—and his relatives as well.

(1) Why did David do what he did for Mephibosheth, rather than killing him?

_____

_____

_____

_____

(2) How would you describe the value of the relationship between David and Mephibosheth's father, Jonathan? What was that relationship worth?

_____

_____

_____

_____

(3) Besides your husband or wife, is there anyone with whom you have a Belt-of-Truth relationship as honorable, righteous, and meaningful as that of David and Jonathan?

_____

_____

_____

AN EXTRA CHALLENGE . . .

Ancient Hebrew covenant is one of the most fascinating biblical subjects you can study, although the Bible itself assumes a basic understanding on the reader's part and therefore does not provide extensive details. The David/Jonathan/Mephibosheth story illustrates some of the basic concepts of salt or friendship covenant, one of four covenants the ancient Hebrews were familiar with. All parties to a salt covenant would agree to share resources with each other's families as needed, and to protect and defend each other through anything that might come.

Salt covenant did not end with death. Each party also agreed to take care of the family of the other party if that person died prematurely. For these reasons David did what he did for Mephibosheth, even though the young man either did not know that David was in covenant with his father or did not know David well enough to know that he would always honor his obligations.

ENTREAT ME NOT TO LEAVE YOU!

To refresh your memory of the Book of Ruth, please read all four uplifting chapters and then answer the following questions:

(1) What happened to Ruth's first husband?

_____

_____

(2) What was the legal relationship between Ruth and Naomi?

_____

_____

(3) What kind of *personal* relationship did Ruth and Naomi have?

_____

(4) What did Ruth do to demonstrate the nature of her relationship with Naomi? Which of her words became oft quoted?

_____

_____

_____

(5) Is there anyone in your life with whom you have a relationship similar to that of Ruth and Naomi? (Such a person need not be an in-law, of course—but certainly could.)

_____

_____

_____

(6) Our modern "Westernized" culture is very different from the culture surrounding Ruth and Naomi. Nevertheless, can you name three positive aspects of our culture that might imitate a Ruth-Naomi relationship?

_____

_____

_____

(7) If we do not have relationships like this today, what do you think tends to inhibit them?

_____

_____

_____

(8) Finally, has God's desired relationship with us changed in any way that would prevent our having Ruth-Naomi relationships?

_____

_____

_____

MAKING THOSE BIBLICAL CONNECTIONS!

The familiar story of Ruth, Naomi, and Boaz contains a direct link to the story of Tamar, Judah's daughter-in-law. This particular Tamar, whose story we looked at in chapter 8, was one of two Tamars in the Bible. The second one was the sister of Absalom, whose story we considered in chapter 2. The first Tamar was forced to resort to trickery to gain for herself a son, directly through Judah, her father-in-law. Indeed, she had twins!

The first of those two sons, Perez, became part of the bloodline that led directly to Christ Himself. The lineage passed through Boaz and Ruth, for Perez was Boaz's great-great-great-great-grandfather. Boaz, of course, was the grandfather of David, from whose direct line our own Savior was born several hundred years later.

The rules governing what was known in that era as Levirate Marriage played a part in both stories. Tamar tried to invoke her right to a male heir through her dead husband's brothers but finally did so through Judah (her father-in-law), as a last resort, because Judah and his sons would not honor their responsibility.

In the case of Boaz and Ruth, Boaz invoked another provision from the same set of laws. After first extending the marriage right to the next-closest male relative (who turned it down for reasons of his own), Boaz invoked his right as the next-closest male relative of Naomi's dead husband in order to marry the surviving wife of Naomi's son. In doing so he ensured that his and Ruth's child (Obed, David's grandfather) would inherit the property that thus "came down" to him through Naomi's husband, their son, and then Boaz as the son's legal replacement. In a very real sense, Boaz thus became the "kinsman redeemer" (goel, in Hebrew) for Naomi, Ruth, and their lineage.

Confused? In the modern age we are not familiar with these ancient provisions for making sure that family possessions stayed within the family and that the women of such families could be cared for in their old age by others from their own families.

FOR SUCH A TIME AS THIS . . .

Another fascinating biblical relationship occurs in the story of Esther, which will be dealt with in greater detail in chapter 12. For now, refer to Esther 2:7 to answer the first two questions below, then to your knowledge of the rest of the Book of Esther for the answer to question #3. (On the other hand, if you cannot answer #3 at this point, hold this question until you have finished chapter 12).

(1) What was the true "family relationship" between Esther and Mordecai?

_____

_____

_____

(2) In reality, however, Mordecai was more like a _____ to Esther.

(3) What might have happened to the Jews if Mordecai had not been able to advise Esther and help her complete her portion of God's larger plan?

_____

_____

_____

THE BREASTPLATE OF RIGHTEOUSNESS

In addition to the Belt of Truth, Paul admonished the Ephesians to strap on the Breastplate of Righteousness. The word "breastplate" has a long and honored history in the Bible. Exodus 28:15–29 gives all the specifications for the original breastplate that God instructed Moses to make in the wilderness for Aaron to wear (along with an ephod, a robe, a tunic, a turban, and a sash) when he ministered before the Lord.

However, that breastplate was designed "for glory and for beauty" (Ex. 28:2, NKJV). In contrast, the breastplate Paul referred to several thousand years later, as worn by the Roman soldiers, was made of heavy leather and was designed to prevent as many blades and projectiles as possible from injuring the heart and lungs of the wearer.

Both of these organs represent the *integrity* of the body and the spirit. Not surprisingly, the word "integrity" occurs more than 20 times in the Bible in the *New King James Version.*

> ### STRAIGHT FROM THE BOOK...
>
> *When you are faced with a decision, an evaluation, a choice, an option, your first thoughts become, Is this in line with God's Word? Am I being presented with the whole truth? Does this in any way violate or contradict my relationship with Jesus as my Savior? Does this conform to the truth of God's love?*

To familiarize yourself with how the Bible treats the concept of personal integrity, please read the following nine verses carefully and see how many you can match with their correct scriptural addresses, *without looking them up first*! Using the numbered list of Scripture references below the quotations, put the correct numbers in front of each quotation. (May I suggest using a pencil rather than a pen at first?) Reflect on the nine examples of integrity in the following verses.

(Hint: This is not an easy exercise! My best advice is to start with the obvious ones. Then, remember that David is considered responsible for the earlier Psalms; not the later ones—so which one sounds most like him?)

___Now if you walk before Me as your father David walked, in **integrity** of heart and in uprightness, to do according to all that I have commanded you, and if you keep My statutes and My judgments,

___Far be it from me that I should say you are right; till I die I will not put away my **integrity** from me.

___The LORD shall judge the peoples; Judge me, O LORD, according to my righteousness, and according to my **integrity** within me.

___Did he not say to me, "She is my sister'? And she, even she herself said, "He is my brother.' In the **integrity** of my heart and innocence of my hands I have done this."

___So he shepherded them according to the **integrity** of his heart, and guided them by the skillfulness of his hands.

___He who walks with **integrity** walks securely, but he who perverts his ways will become known.

___ in all things showing yourself to be a pattern of good works; in doctrine showing **integrity**, reverence, incorruptibility,

___Then the LORD said to Satan, "Have you considered My servant Job, that there is none like him on the earth, a blameless and upright man, one who fears God and shuns evil? And still he holds fast to his **integrity**, although you incited Me against him, to destroy him without cause."

___The righteous man walks in his **integrity**; his children are blessed after him.

(1) Titus 2:7
(2) Proverbs 20:7
(3) 1 Kings 9:4
(4) Job 2:3
(5) Genesis 20:5
(6) Psalm 7:8
(7) Job 27:5
(8) Proverbs 10:9
(9) Psalm 78:72

THE SHOES OF PREPARATION OF THE GOSPEL OF PEACE

The Roman soldiers also wore heavy shoes that were really boots, the soles of which were often equipped with pieces of metal to ensure a solid grip on the ground. When Paul says "having shod your feet with the preparation of the gospel of peace" (Eph. 6:15) he is referring to a solid foundation that would not waffle or waver.

To illustrate this concept biblically, rather than referring you to a series of stories about heroes who stood firm for God, let's work through the following table. Begin by looking up the Scripture reference in the first column. In the next column, indicate who the verse is talking about. In the final column, from your knowledge of that person's story (or from reading the surrounding verses in context), indicate with a "yes" or a "no" whether that person (or persons) *stood firm* in obedience to God, during a time of testing.

Scripture	Person(s)	Stood Firm?
(1) Luke 22:3		
(2) Judges 11:30–34		
(3) Numbers 14:6–9		
(4) Acts 5:1–5		
(5) Matthew 19:16–22		
(6) Daniel 6:4–23		
(7) Genesis 19:17, 26		
(8) Exodus 32:19, 20		
(9) Mark 14:72		
(10) Genesis 22:9–13		

BRINGING IT ALL TOGETHER . . .

God is certainly capable of bringing about whatever He wants to happen, with no help from us. However, even as He encourages us to have righteous, productive relationships with each other, He prefers to work through relationships with us, *whenever and wherever* His people are truly willing to fit into His plans and work with Him.

For one final time, let's review the stories we have already examined in this chapter, plus consider additional stories. After reading the passage, answer the questions that follow.

STORIES TO REVIEW AND TO CONSIDER . . .

(1) Joseph, who interpreted the dreams of the Pharaoh of Egypt (Gen. 41:14–39)

(2) Ruth, whose marriage to Boaz came about because of his family connections to—and Ruth's friendship with—Naomi (The Book of Ruth)

(3) Esther, who was able to outmaneuver Haman, using the advice of her uncle, Mordecai (The Book of Esther)

(4) Nehemiah, who built a relationship with Artaxerxes (sometimes called Xerxes), and then petitioned him to allow the Jews to return from captivity and rebuild Jerusalem (Neh. 2:1–6)

Now, name the one *vital historical fact* that all four of these stories about *important relationships* contributed to. (Hint: The preservation of what?)

_____

_____

_____

_____

What can we also conclude about God Himself? What is one of the main qualities that He has possessed since before creation began? (Hint: The correct answer could very well evolve out of our discussion of the Breastplate of Righteousness. In other words, what personal quality that is linked to the breastplate does God require of us?)

_____

_____

_____

_____

CHECKLIST "STRAIGHT FROM THE BOOK"

Now, read the following checklist "straight from the book" and answer the questions for yourself. Or, if you are in a group, have someone read the list aloud while everyone else answers silently:

_____ Do you exhale vehement hate or profound love?

_____ Do you exhale cynicism and sarcasm or appreciation and praise?

_____ Do you exhale an attitude of bitterness or of gratefulness?

_____ Do you exhale anger and pain or the healing balm of kindness?

_____ Do you exhale revenge or mercy?

_____ Do you exhale seething silence or a vulnerable willingness to reach out to others?

_____ Do you give reluctantly and stingily or quickly and generously?

_____ Do you respond with an air of pride or with humility?

_____ Do you fear and distrust others, or are you open and eager to receive their good ideas?

Finally, based on what you've gleaned from this chapter, in what ways do you feel you can learn to *stand firm*, maintain your *integrity*, and both broaden and improve your *relationships* with others to become a better servant of the Lord? Write your answer below. Be honest! In fact, if you are working as part of a study group, decide for yourself whether you wish to share this answer with others.

_____

_____

_____

_____

_____

STRAIGHT FROM THE BOOK . . .

We need to see clearly the character of a person, because truth telling and living in truth are vital to the success of any friendship, business partnership, marriage, or any other relationship that is linked to long-term godly goals.

WORDS TO REMEMBER . . .

Finally, my brethren, be strong in the Lord and in the power of His might. Put on the whole armor of God that you may be able to stand against the wiles of the devil. For we do not wrestle against flesh and blood, but against principalities, against powers, against the rulers of the darkness of this age, against spiritual hosts of wickedness in the heavenly places. Therefore take up the whole armor of God, that you may be able to withstand in the evil day, and having done all, to stand (Eph. 6:10–13, NKJV).

CLOSING PRAYER . . .

Our Father, we entreat You now to help us develop our own integrity like that of David and Job. Help us also to develop honest, caring relationships with the people around, as honorable as those of Ruth and Naomi. May we also to be grounded in Your Word, and may we increase our faith daily in our walk with You.
In Jesus' name, Amen.

STRAIGHT FROM THE BOOK . . .

Just as we are the ones who determine what we will allow into our lives, so, too, we are the ones who determine whether we will seek daily to be cleansed of sin and to pursue the will of God.

10

———⁓———

"Taking Up" Armor

I once had a conversation with a man whose children were attending a Vacation Bible School sponsored by my church. He was smiling over a picture of a Roman soldier that his young son had brought home. The soldier was dressed in the Roman armor referred to by the apostle Paul in his discussion of *spiritual* armor (Eph. 6:14–20).

"It's all so out-of-date," he said. "No one wears this kind of thing anymore! No one fights the way the people who wore this armor fought. Everything is impersonal; from a distance; even *surgical* and *sanitary*. You need to find an illustration that my kids can relate to—something *modern*; something that reflects the way we do things today."

One of the problems with this man's logic is that the spiritual enemy who attacks us today is the same one who attacked Adam and Eve, David and Saul, Judas and Peter, and all the other millions of people who have served the Lord throughout the centuries. Granted, we now live in a world of computers, cell phones, and high-tech warfare, but Satan still attacks with his effective tolls and methods.

If anything, the spiritual armor Paul talked about is even more essential today. Modern technology, connecting us to the unsaved world in ever-more-clever and amazing ways, also gives the devil just that many more opportunities to connect with us him.

So, let's look at the three remaining parts of Paul's *Armor of God* to see if we can figure out how to use them today to defend ourselves against the evils of Satan *even more effectively* than some of the people of Paul's time were able to do.

THE SHIELD OF FAITH

It isn't difficult to understand how a handheld shield can protect a soldier from knives and arrows. The Roman shields were made of heavy leather and were often doused in water to neutralize fiery arrows.[2] This treatment had the added advantage of making the leather even tougher when it dried. After one or two thorough soakings, it would get as hard and unbending as iron.

> ### STRAIGHT FROM THE BOOK . . .
>
> *When you are strong in faith, filled with hope, and keenly aware of the Holy Spirit's presence and power, you are not going to fall victim to the devil's fiery darts of temptation or crumble and wither under the devil's attacks! You are going to win the battle every time.*

Paul equates the Roman shield with our own *Shield of Faith*, meant to be our first line of defense against the enemy and also prone to "toughening up" with use. "For by grace you have been saved through faith and that not of yourselves; it is the gift of God" (Eph. 2:8, NKJV) said Paul just four chapters earlier.

WHAT IS THIS THING CALLED "FAITH"?

We all have our favorite stories that demonstrate "faith." One of mine involves a man who grew up in the Midwest and gave his heart to Christ in his late teens.

This young man was highly intelligent, but he was born with a reading disability (a form of dyslexia) that made it very difficult for him to read fluently. This limitation affected his educational opportunities. When he was growing up, neither scientist nor educator knew much about how the brain really worked and even less about how to help people with these kinds of difficulties.

▼

▼

One day his church sponsored a mission's outreach and asked for annual pledges from the congregation. The young man pledged $3,000, in a day when that much money would buy a new car and pay the rent for six months.

The next day his pastor came to see him. "Surely you meant $30.00," he said. "And that's okay—we'll be happy to move the period." "No, no. I meant exactly what I wrote," the young man replied. "God told me to put down that number. I don't know what He has in store, but I have a whole year to find out!"

During the next year, when it came time to pay on his pledge, the young man always seemed to have the money. He got a bonus; he was asked to work overtime; unexpectedly he got a second job on the weekends.

On the day he made the last payment on his pledge he felt the Lord telling him to follow his dream and start his own construction company, even though he knew nothing about running a business and needed help to read the forms. However, he did what he felt God was telling him to do. The rest—as they say—is history!

I talked to him about 15 years later. In his own words, from the very first day, "The windows of heaven opened up and the blessings poured out!" The young man made so much money he was able to employ a huge labor force (including a secretary to read all his mail) and spread the wealth around. That's not all—he gave the major share of it away, to missions, to the local needy—to anyone he knew of who needed help.

And, of course, he has never forgotten what brought all this to him. Faith, like what Jesus spoke about in Matthew 17:20. The young man had faith, he acted on it, and God responded.

What is this "faith," this "gift of God"? How does it work? How do we claim it and develop it, and how do we use it to defend ourselves?

Perhaps the best-known discussion of faith in the Bible can be found in the eleventh chapter of Hebrews—the famous "faith chapter." It begins with these familiar words:

"Now faith is the substance of things hoped for, the evidence of things not seen" (Heb. 11:1, NKJV).

Experts do not agree on who the author of Hebrews might have been, but no one disputes its authenticity. Hebrews mentions several examples of outstanding men and women of faith in the Bible, some of them well-known (e.g., Enoch, Noah, Abraham and Isaac; Sarah, et al) and some not so familiar. I urge you to read and study the entire chapter for yourself.

Meanwhile, let's consider just one of the "Heroes of the Faith" from that chapter—one mentioned but not really discussed. Turn to Judges 11 and try reading the whole chapter, especially the background material in the beginning. Here are the first three verses, with fill-in blanks to help you focus on the material:

Now Jephthah the Gileadite was a mighty man of valor, but he was the son of a _____; and Gilead begot Jephthah. Gilead's wife bore sons; and when his wife's sons grew up, they _____ Jephthah out, and said to him, "You shall have no _____ in our father's house, for you are the son of another woman." Then Jephthah fled from his brothers and dwelt in the land of Tob; and worthless men banded together with Jephthah and went out _____ with him (Judg. 11:1–3, NKJV).

❧Based on these verses, what two things do we know, about Jephthah's *birth* and his *early years*, which probably would have disqualified him from serving God in any official, man-sanctioned leadership role?

(1) _____

(2) _____

❧Next, notice what the elders of Jephthah's region of Israel did in the next three verses, when they found themselves in trouble. No questions on this section; just read it and note the irony!

It came to pass after a time that the people of Ammon made war against Israel. And so it was, when the people of Ammon made war against Israel, that the elders of Gilead went to get Jephthah from the land of Tob. Then they said to Jephthah, "Come and be our _____ that we may fight against the people of Ammon" (Judg. 11:4–6, NKJV).

Next, Jephthah asks why the men of Gilead had the nerve to come to him for help after throwing him out of their region, through no fault of his own. He then gets a guarantee from them, that if he agrees to help them he will be completely in charge (vv. 7–10). Then, even as he attempts to talk the king of the Ammonites out of fighting he also gives us a history lesson about why the Ammonites' quarrel with the Children of Israel should never have come about in the first place.

Finally, in verses 29–31, we come to the famous *Vow of Faith* that Jephthah made to the Lord before he went into battle:

Then the Spirit of the LORD came upon Jephthah, and he passed through Gilead and Manasseh, and passed through Mizpah of Gilead; and from Mizpah of Gilead he advanced toward the people of Ammon. And Jephthah made a vow to the LORD, and said, "If You will indeed _____ the people of Ammon into my hands, it will be that whatever comes out of the doors of my house to _____ me, when I _____ in peace from the people of Ammon, shall surely be the LORD's, and I will offer it up as a burnt offering" (Judg. 11:29–31, NKJV).

(1) In your opinion, was Jephthah's vow a bit rash?

_____

_____

(2) If not, why not?

_____

_____

(3) Either way, why would he have made that vow? In essence, what did he agree to give up to God, and what did that "price" represent to him?

_____

_____

To find out how the story ends, read *Handel and the "Musical Connection"* featured in this section. Also, complete your study of Judges 11 by reading verses 32–40, and then answer the questions.

(1) Did God require Jephthah to make the pledge he made?

_____

_____

_____

(2) Whose idea was it?

_____

_____

_____

(3) Did God approve? Either way, how do you know?

_____

_____

_____

(4) Does God require us to make life-and-death pledges to Him to "earn" His help?

_____

_____

_____

(5) If you answered "no," why did Jephthah do it? And if you said earlier that God approved of Jephthah's vow, why would that be true?

_____

_____

_____

(6) How do Jephthah's actions demonstrate his faith in God?

_____

_____

_____

(7) Did Jephthah's willingness to "sacrifice" his daughter, even though that was not his original intention, indicate greater or lesser faith in God? Why?

_____

_____

_____

HANDEL AND THE "MUSICAL CONNECTION"

George Frederic Handel is well-known for his inspired oratorio, Messiah, a musical rendering of the story of Christ's birth, death, and resurrection. Most large cities feature one or more year-end performances of at least the first two (Christmas) sections, often including portions from the third (Easter) section as well—which contains the great "Hallelujah Chorus."

Messiah is only one of several operas and oratorios written by Handel on biblical subjects. Handel's baroque musical style (heavy on ornamentation; very difficult to sing) is not always in favor with modern audiences, but the stories themselves (though often distorted for dramatic effect) are always fascinating and uplifting. So it is with Jephthah, featuring the dilemma Jephthah faced when it came time to honor his vow to the Lord. A beautiful aria from the score, called "Waft her, angels," has Jephthah praying that God would honor and protect his innocent daughter.

▼

129

▼

The question many people ask, both about the opera libretto (i.e., "little book") and about the biblical text it's based on, is whether Jephthah really offered up his own daughter, literally, as a burnt sacrifice. Most authorities do not think so, including the translators of the New King James Version of the Bible (see the last sentence of Judg. 11:39). Instead, Jephthah fulfilled his vow by requiring her never to marry, thus bringing the equivalent of "death by deprivation" to a young woman in a culture that valued marriage, children, and family above all else—thus the daughter's period of mourning prior to her acceptance of Jephthah's decision, as detailed in Judges 11:36–40.

SPEAKING OF FAITH . . .

Down through the centuries, the word faith has been defined in many different ways by many different people. One of my favorites is not so much a definition as an extension of the concept.

"Faith," this one says, "is passive; the active counterpart is trust. When you move from having faith in God to putting your trust in God and begin doing tangible things as a result, you've moved into a whole new dimension. You don't move to a foreign country and minister to those who have never heard of Jesus Christ 'on faith.' You do it 'in trust.' Faith is hopeful and involves waiting on the Lord. Trust is bold and certain and involves acting as He leads you, not waiting for Him to lead you."

THE HELMET OF SALVATION

In First Thessalonians 5:8, Paul says:

> But let us who are of the day be sober, putting on the breast-plate of faith and love, and as a helmet the hope of salvation (NKJV).

This definition adds to the more familiar reference by Paul in

Ephesians 6:17 (see "Words to Remembers" at the end of this chapter). Both references refer to an earlier one from Isaiah 59:17:

> For He put on righteousness as a breastplate,
> And a helmet of salvation on His head . . . (NKJV).

What makes this verse from Isaiah especially meaningful is that Isaiah was talking about God Himself in the person of Jesus Christ as the Redeemer of Zion putting the helmet of salvation on His *own head*. Should we do any less? If we do, should we expect any less than what God promises at the conclusion of this prophecy just a few verses later:

> As for Me," says the LORD, "this is My covenant with them: My Spirit who is upon you, and My words which I have put in your mouth, shall not depart from your mouth, nor from the mouth of your descendants, nor from the mouth of your descendants' descendants," says the LORD, "from this time and forevermore" (Is. 59:21, NKJV).

The key, of course, is to recognize that our own salvation, by virtue of Christ's death on the Cross, is eternal and cannot be taken away. The devil will certainly try, and he will come at us with every possible weapon, trick, and device he can muster. If you wear the Helmet of Salvation and always remember this *Jesus is our Savior*, the devil cannot possibly prevail.

> ## STRAIGHT FROM THE BOOK . . .
>
> *Little faith says, "God can do this."*
> *Great faith says, "God will do this."*
> *Great faith says, "It's as good as done."*

✎ Read the verses below and then answer the questions that follow.

Ephesians 5:23b

Christ is head of the church; and He is the Savior of the body [i.e., the church] (NKJV).

Psalm 7:10

My defense is of God, who saves the upright in heart (NKJV).

Ephesians 1:7

In Him we have redemption through His blood, the forgiveness of sins, according to the riches of His grace . . . (NKJV).

Acts 15:11

But we believe that through the grace of the Lord Jesus Christ we shall be saved in the same manner as they" (NKJV).

Ephesians 2:5

. . . even when we were dead in trespasses, made us alive together with Christ (by grace you have been saved), . . . (NKJV).

Ephesians 2:8

For by grace you have been saved through faith, and that not of yourselves; it is the gift of God, . . . (NKJV).

2 Thessalonians 2:16

Now may our Lord Jesus Christ Himself, and our God and Father, who has loved us and given us everlasting consolation and good hope by grace, . . . (NKJV).

Romans 3:24

. . . being justified freely by His grace through the redemption that is in Christ Jesus, . . . (NKJV).

Titus 3:7

. . . that having been justified by His grace we should become heirs according to the hope of eternal life (NKJV).

QUESTIONS ON THE PASSAGES . . .

(1) Where does our salvation come from?

_____

_____

_____

(2) By what means, or "mechanism"?

_____

_____

(3) Can we earn it on our own?

_____

_____

(4) Can we lose it by failing to deserve it?

_____

(5) Is it therefore temporary or permanent?

_____

_____

(6) Can Satan take it away?

_____

_____

(7) What should we tell him if he tries?

_____

_____

(8) What verse(s) should we quote to him?

_____

_____

(9) Who else quoted Bible verses to Satan?

_____

_____

(10) What was the result?

_____

_____

(11) Are we smarter than He (#9) is?

_____

_____

(12) Should we not, then, do the same?

_____

_____

(13) Have you started yet?

_____

_____

STRAIGHT FROM THE BOOK . . .

When you put on the full armor of God, you say to the devil, "You have to go through Jesus to get to me! You may launch fiery darts against me. You may assault my mind with your temptations, doubts, fears, and lies. But you cannot defeat me. I am in Christ and He is in me, and there is nothing you can do to touch or destroy my security in Him.

THE SWORD OF THE SPIRIT

If you survived the previous exercise and answered "yes" to number 13, in addition to putting on the Helmet of Salvation and _asserting the certainty of your salvation_, you have already begun to wield the _Sword of the Spirit_—the Word of God. Preferably, you keep it not in your Bible bag (the modern sheath or scabbard) but in your heart and in your mind where it can do the most good.

Memorizing the Word of God

The ancient Hebrews studied the Word of God by memorizing it. They memorized it not by bland repetition, but by setting it to music via a system of symbols inserted above the Hebrew text. Even today, Jewish cantors use the same system when they "cant," or sing, what we know as the "Old Testament" but which they call the Tanakh.

Each symbol, or "trope," positioned every few words, signifies a particular melody to which the next batch of words should be sung. Over the centuries a number of different melodies—corresponding to each of the trope markers—have evolved among different Jewish traditions. The two main strains of modern times are Ashkenazi (European) and Sephardic (centered in the Iberian Peninsula, which includes Spain and Portugal). Within each of these broad families a number of variations still exist.

Ancient rabbis (teachers) who memorized the entire Old Testament were called gaons. Perhaps from this, via the Latin root, comes our modern English word, genius—and indeed, to many of us unaccustomed to memorizing large portions of text, it would seem to require a genius to memorize the entire Old Testament! The apostle Paul, himself a rabbi of the Pharisees (Phil. 3:5), was one of the best-known gaons. This memorizing strategy explains why he can say with such authority "It is written" so frequently in his own writings.

To help you become familiar with the verses you need for your own defense, I have constructed the following "Table of Vices and Virtues." It's based on the traditional Seven Deadly Vices sometimes talked about in secular literature, but with a twist. I have listed the seven vices in the column to the left. In the next column I have listed the opposite (opposing) virtues. For example, the opposite of pride is humility, which honors God rather than offending Him. Thus, the first column shows what you want to avoid, while the second column shows what you want to develop and exhibit instead.

You can devise a couple of activities for this table: (1) make a larger copy of the table below (2) re-create it on your computer, developing it on-screen. Don't limit yourself to the seven vices I've listed. If you are plagued by others, list them. Then figure out what the opposing virtues would be and list those, too.

(3) Using a good concordance (or Bible software if you have that available and prefer to work on the computer), build a list of verses that you can *memorize*, then *quote out loud* to the devil whenever he tempts you to indulge in anything you know is not pleasing to the Lord. Search under both the vices and the virtues (and their synonyms as well) to find appropriate verses. You will find a huge treasure chest of resources within the Bible.

This exercise should become a labor of love, with emphasis on the word *labor* so the resulting benefits will be truly yours. (4) Additionally, you could work on building your own list (or table) with others in a group setting.

For optimal application your list will become your own tool and not something better-suited to other people. You are honing your own sword. You can't use someone else's when the battle swirls around you.

You are developing a very *powerful arsenal of anti-Satan weaponry* if you pursue this exercise.

Vice	Opposing Virtue	Scriptural Helps
Pride	Humility	
Greed	Generosity	
Envy	Love	
Anger	Kindness	
Lust	Self-Control	
Gluttony	Temperance	
Laziness	Zeal	

Virtue by Definition . . .

To help you identify areas in which you could build your "scriptural arsenal," take a look at the following list:

Pride/Humility. *Humility requires us to see ourselves as we are and not by comparing ourselves to others. Pride and vanity are competitive. If someone else's pride really bothers you, you could have a lot of it yourself.*

Greed/Generosity. *This area is about more than money. Generosity can mean letting others get the credit or praise. It can mean giving without expecting something back. Greed wants to get its "fair share" or a bit more; generosity wants to give its fair share—or a bit more.*

Envy/Love. *"Love is patient, love is kind . . ." Love actively seeks the good of others for their sake. Envy resents the good others receive or even might receive. At times, envy is almost indistinguishable from pride.*

Anger/Kindness. *Kindness means taking the tender approach, with patience and compassion. Anger is often our first reaction to the problems of others. Impatience with the faults of others is related to this characteristic.*

Lust/Self-Control. *Self-control and self-mastery prevent pleasure from killing the soul by suffocation. Legitimate pleasures are controlled in the same way an athlete's muscles are—for maximum efficiency without damage. Lust is the self-destructive drive for pleasure out of proportion to its worth.*

Gluttony/Temperance. *Temperance accepts the natural limits of pleasures and preserves this natural balance. It pertains not only to food but to entertainment and other legitimate goods, and even to the company of others.*

Laziness/Zeal. *Zeal is the energetic response of the heart to God's commands. Other sins work together to deaden the spiritual senses so we first become slow to respond to God and then drift completely into the sleep of complacency.*

FINAL THOUGHTS . . .

Putting on your spiritual armor establishes your identity in Christ. By giving Him your faith and trust, you get His protection against all those fiery darts of the devil.

It's important to understand *how* He works *through* you to strengthen and protect you. Always, your walk with the Lord is a partnership. Once you begin to put your armor on, He begins helping you *develop* it and *use* it more effectively. God is in charge, gently challenging, teaching, and lovingly disciplining His children. He will supply everything you need, but in return He requires you to participate in your own *growth*, *education*, and *defense*.

God could literally "do it all, all the time," but He partners *with* us rather than simply doing it *for* us. In that way He continually models the kind of relationships He would like us to have with each other. That approach makes our gains and our victories all the more meaningful and complete. We have all seen spoiled children, with no sense of gratitude or responsibility, because they have been given everything they could possibly want with nothing required of them in return.

God is the perfect Father with a perfect understanding of what we need to do to be strong and righteous—and safe—in His embrace.

WORDS TO REMEMBER . . .

Stand therefore, having girded your waist with truth, having put on the breastplate of righteousness, and having shod your feet with the preparation of the gospel of peace; above all, taking the shield of faith with which you will be able to quench all the fiery darts of the wicked one. And take the helmet of salvation, and the sword of the Spirit, which is the word of God; praying always with all prayer and supplication in the Spirit, being watchful to this end with all perseverance and supplication for all the saints—and for me, that utterance may be given to me, that I may open my mouth boldly to make known the mystery of the gospel, for which I am an ambassador in chains; that in it I may speak boldly, as I ought to speak (Eph. 6:14–20, NKJV).

Closing Prayer . . .

Our Father, help us to "take up" daily the armor that You have provided—the Shield of Faith, the Helmet of Salvation, and the Sword of the Spirit. Help us to increase our faith, be secure in our salvation, and study Your Word until it becomes truly a mighty sword in our hands.

In Jesus' name, Amen.

11

—⌇—

STANDING STRONG IN PRAYER

I have never met anyone who believed that he could maintain a friendship with someone else without making regular contact. Whether by mail, e-mail, telephone, or conversations in person, you must have some kind of regular exchange with your friend, or you will eventually lose all the practical aspects of that friendship—the things that keep it going.

Also, when you lose regular contact, you will find it very hard to go to that same person for support when trouble hits, even if he or she is the only person you've ever known with the resources to help you out. The reason is quite simple. People are connected to each other through *relationships*, and like automobiles and airplanes and anything else that might move us forward, relationships require regular maintenance.

Most people understand this, yet we seem to have difficulty in applying the basic rules of relationship to our connection with God. We seem to have little understanding of how an ongoing, personal relationship with Him actually works.

> ### STRAIGHT FROM THE BOOK . . .
>
> *One of the main reasons that so many believers in Christ are weak is that they do not pray when the devil attacks them. Prayer is not a piece of spiritual armor against the devil. Prayer is what we do once we are clothed in the armor that is the identity of Jesus.*

THE POWER OF PRAYER

Just for a moment, think again about one or two points we have already made. In previous chapters we saw several examples of how we must depend on God through faith. At the same time we know that we are to put on the armor of God to protect ourselves from sin. Obviously the two go together—*you do your part* by using the tools and protections that God provides then trust Him for the rest.

In a sense, prayer works exactly the same way. If you want God's best in your life, you have to keep the lines of communication open so you can hear and feel—so you can *experience*—His daily guidance! A ten-year-old boy listens to his father's voice when he is learning to ride a bicycle, but how can the father instruct and reassure the boy if the two have not talked to each other for months? How can they both know, from their history, how the relationship between them actually works?

THE BIBLE SAYS A LOT ABOUT PRAYER!

The word *pray* occurs about 140 times in the *New King James Version* of the Bible. It appears for the very first time in the 20th chapter of Genesis. Consider what happened in Genesis 20:1–7.

> And Abraham journeyed from there to the South, and _____ between Kadesh and Shur, and stayed in Gerar. Now Abraham said of Sarah his wife, "She is my _____." And Abimelech king of Gerar sent and took Sarah. But God came to Abimelech in a dream by night, and said to him, "Indeed you are a dead man because of the woman whom you have taken, for she is a man's wife."
>
> But Abimelech had not come near her; and he said, "Lord, will You slay a righteous nation also? Did he not say to me, "She is my sister"? And she, even she herself said, "He is my brother.' In the integrity of my heart and _____ of my hands I have done this."

And God said to him in a dream, "Yes, I know that you did this in the integrity of your heart. For I also withheld you from sinning against Me; therefore I did not let you touch her. Now therefore, restore the man's wife; for he is a prophet, and he will _____ for you and you shall _____. But if you do not restore her, know that you shall surely die, you and all who are yours" (NKJV).

(1) According to all you have read and heard about the origins of God's chosen people, what person in this story undoubtedly had the closest, most vital, ongoing relationship with God?

_____

_____

(2) Given that, whom would you expect God to be most concerned with protecting? To put it another way, to whom did God want Sarah restored, and why?

_____

_____

(3) Another way of thinking about this passage is to ask yourself if God had a higher stake in defending one party over the other. Does God have an equal stake in all of our lives?

_____

_____

_____

(4) What might have happened if Abimelech had refused to obey God? What do you think about that possibility? From God's perspective, what would justify it?

_____

_____

_____

(5) In order to resolve this situation what did God require besides Abimelech's agreement to restore Sarah to Abraham? In other words, Abimelech had to do something as well. What did God say that Abraham, the prophet, would also do so that Abimelech could live?

_____

_____

(6) What does all this suggest about the value and importance of prayer in all our dealings with God?

_____

_____

A Privilege and a Requirement!

The number one condition that Satan wants to create in your life is *prayerlessness.* Satan knows that a healthy prayer life can do great things for you. In contrast, he knows that failure to pray on a regular basis leads to exactly the opposite condition. The path he would have you take leads through *burden bearing,* which leads to *weariness* and eventually to spiritual *weakness.*

> ### Straight from the Book . . .
>
> *The devil knows far better than most human beings just how potent prayer is and how directly prayer is related to his destruction! The devil knows that we are the most vulnerable to his attack when we don't pray.*

No wonder God gave us so many wonderful promises regarding prayer—He knew exactly what we would be up against! For example, read Second Chronicles 7:14 and fill in the blanks below:

. . . if My people who are called by My name will _____ themselves, and pray and _____ _____ _____, and turn from their _____ _____, then I will hear from heaven, and will _____ forgive their sin and _____ heal their land (NKJV).

These oft-remembered words were given by God to Solomon during the night following the dedication of the temple. In them . . .

(1) What four things did God ask the Children of Israel to do?

_____

_____

_____

(2) What two things did God promise to do in return?

_____

_____

_____

(3) Even though these words were spoken many centuries ago, are they just as true for us today as they were when God gave them to Solomon?

_____

_____

_____

Two generations earlier, one of the godliest men of the Bible also said something profound about prayer at what was probably the most difficult moment of his life. Samuel was the last of the judges to lead the Children of Israel in the years following the death of Moses. Eventually they insisted on a king, and after a time God gave them Saul *even though He knew that an earthly king would not be good for them*. Read First Samuel 12:23, fill in the blanks below, and see what Samuel said at Saul's coronation.

Moreover, as for me, far be it from me that I should _____ against the LORD in ceasing to pray for you; but I will teach you the good and the right way (NKJV).

(1) What did Samuel acknowledge that he would be doing if he failed to continue praying for the Children of Israel,

even though he disagreed with the decision they'd made about their own future leadership?

_____

_____

(2) What does this say about our obligation to God? Is prayer optional—something we should do only when we feel like it? In the space below, answer these questions and add anything you think is important. Tell how you feel, personally, about the proper role of prayer in your life!

_____

_____

PERSONAL REASONS FOR NOT PRAYING

If you feel that you are not praying directly to God as much as you'd like to, use the following spaces to create a list of things that might be keeping you from regular communion with God. Typical reasons include over over-involvement in a job or in other evening and weekend activities, too much time spent on entertainment, and a general feeling that prayer _doesn't do any good_—which, of course, sets up a self-fulfilling, self-defeating prophesy!

Be honest with yourself, and if you need more than ten spaces, add additional lines.

    (1) _____

    (2) _____

    (3) _____

    (4) _____

    (5) _____

    (6) _____

    (7) _____

    (8) _____

    (9) _____

   (10) _____

THE PRAYER OF A KING

The Bible contains many of David's prayers, especially in the Psalms. Below is one of his prayers that might not be quite as familiar to you. This prayer is David's response to the time God sent the prophet Nathan with His personal promise to build and maintain David's house forever.

> For You, O LORD of hosts, God of Israel, have revealed this to Your servant, saying, "I will build you a house.' Therefore Your servant has found it in his heart to pray this prayer to You.
>
> "And now, O Lord GOD, You are God, and Your words are true, and You have promised this goodness to Your servant. Now therefore, let it please You to bless the house of Your servant, that it may continue before You forever; for You, O Lord GOD, have spoken it, and with Your blessing let the house of Your servant be blessed forever" (2 Sam. 7:27–29, NKJV).

(1) Consider the back-and-forth dynamic of this little-heard prayer. For example, according to David's words, who took the initiative in this exchange—that is, who did the first thing?

_____

_____

(2) What did He do?

_____

_____

(3) What was David's immediate response?

_____

_____

STRAIGHT FROM THE BOOK . . .

❑ *Your understanding of the Word of God is in direct proportion to your prayers.*

❑ *Your holiness and righteousness are directly related to your prayers.*

❑ *Your fruitfulness and usefulness to God are directly related to your prayers.*

HOW TO BE EFFECTIVE IN PRAYER

Among other things, David's prayer satisfied several of the requirements of effective prayer. Based on the following criteria for effective prayer,

(1) Be specific and well-defined

(2) Listen for God to speak to you

(3) Pray about everything

(4) Pray and intercede in the spirit

(5) Pray with faith

how did David do? Well . . .

(1) David's prayer was certainly specific and well-defined.

(2) David certainly listened for God to speak—indeed, he prayed as a direct result of a word that came *straight from* God, through Nathan.

(3) David did not pray about "everything" in this particular prayer, but we know that over the course of time he almost certainly did pray about every aspect of his personal life and his kingly responsibilities. The goal is to be specific and well-defined *with respect to each individual item in each individual prayer.*

Beyond that, the goal is to pray "about every individual thing" in its proper turn.

However, we can't do all of this praying all at the same time. We're all familiar with the person who is asked to pray *specifically* over an offering and then proceeds to pray for missions, new converts, the pastor's sermon, the sick, and the upcoming revival as well. None of this is *wrong*; it just doesn't fit that particular occasion!)

(4) David was definitely praying as he was led by the Holy Spirit.

(5) David definitely prayed "with faith," for the faith he demonstrated over and over again was obviously among his strengths.

What a joy-inducing, spirit-lifting, worship-generating, spiritually-energizing blessing from God!

DO WE HEAR FROM PROPHETS TODAY?

Contrary to the experiences of David, Saul, and the other kings of Israel, in our day we tend not to hear directly from God through His prophets anywhere near as often. Some might say this is true because we are not "kings" in the same sense, with responsibility over the entire body of God's chosen people. While true, this story does not end there.

Why does God no longer need to send people whom He has specifically chosen to deliver His messages? Probably the biggest reason is that ever since the Day of Pentecost (and as promised by Christ Himself in John 14:26), when we accept salvation through Jesus Christ, the Holy Spirit comes to reside within our spirit. Thus, each of us has a direct link to God through His divine, all-day/all-night presence within us.

Incidentally, the New King James Version of the Bible makes 110 references to the Holy Spirit, most of them in the above context and most of them (101, to be exact) in the New Testament.

RECOGNIZING EFFECTIVE PRAYERS

The following verses all contain the word pray, along with instruction or a comment about our need—that is, our requirement—to pray, in various situations. Read each verse and then record (in the columns marked "X") the number of all the characteristics of effective prayer that apply to each verse from the "How to Be Effective in Prayer" list. The goal is not to see how many verses get a perfect score but to read and think about just a few of the many biblical verses that admonish us to pray, and often tell us how.

Verse	X	Verse	X
Matt. 5:44 - But I say to you, love your enemies, bless those who curse you, do good to those who hate you, and pray for those who spitefully use you and persecute you (NKJV).		**Matt. 6:6** - But you, when you pray, go into your room, and when you have shut your door, pray to your Father who is in the secret place; and your Father who sees in secret will reward you openly (NKJV).	
Mark 14:38 - Watch and pray, lest you enter into temptation. The spirit indeed is willing, but the flesh is weak" (NKJV).		**Luke 6:28** - bless those who curse you, and pray for those who spitefully use you (NKJV).	
Luke 10:2 - Then He said to them, "The harvest truly is great, but the laborers are few; therefore pray the Lord of the harvest to send out laborers into His harvest (NKJV).		**Luke 11:2** - So He said to them, "When you pray, say: Our Father in heaven, Hallowed be Your name. Your kingdom come. Your will be done On earth as it is in heaven (NKJV).	
Luke 18:1 - Then He spoke a parable to them, that men always ought to pray and not lose heart (NKJV).		**Luke 21:36** - Watch therefore, and pray always that you may be counted worthy to escape all these things that will come to pass, and to stand before the Son of Man" (NKJV).	

Verse	X	Verse	X
Luke 22:46 - Then He said to them, "Why do you sleep? Rise and pray, lest you enter into temptation" (NKJV).		**Acts 8:24** - Then Simon answered and said, "Pray to the Lord for me, that none of the things which you have spoken may come upon me" (NKJV).	
2 Cor. 13:9 - For we are glad when we are weak and you are strong. And this also we pray, that you may be made complete (NKJV).		**Phil. 1:9** - And this I pray, that your love may abound still more and more in knowledge and all discernment (NKJV).	
Col. 1:9 - For this reason we also, since the day we heard it, do not cease to pray for you, and to ask that you may be filled with the knowledge of His will in all wisdom and spiritual understanding (NKJV).		**1 Thess. 5:17** - Pray without ceasing (NKJV).	
2 Thess. 3:1 - Finally, brethren, pray for us, that the word of the Lord may run swiftly and be glorified, just as it is with you (NKJV).		**1 Tim. 2:1** - Therefore I exhort first of all that supplications, prayers, intercessions, and giving of thanks be made for all men (NKJV).	
1 Tim. 2:8 - I desire therefore that the men pray everywhere, lifting up holy hands, without wrath and doubting; (NKJV)		**James 5:13** - Is anyone among you suffering? Let him pray. Is anyone cheerful? Let him sing psalms (NKJV).	
James 5:14 - Is anyone among you sick? Let him call for the elders of the church, and let them pray over him, anointing him with oil in the name of the Lord (NKJV).		**James 5:16** - Confess your trespasses to one another, and pray for one another, that you may be healed. The effective, fervent prayer of a righteous man avails much (NKJV).	

THE BENEFITS OF PRAYING

The benefits of a healthy prayer life include discernment, self-awareness of sin, and renewed energy and strength—always of spiritual energy but often of physical energy as well. The best possible way to improve your relationship with the Lord is to increase the focus and the frequency of your prayer times with Him.

WORDS TO REMEMBER . . .

The spirit also helps in our weaknesses. For we do not know what we should pray for as we ought, but the Spirit Himself makes intercession for us with groanings which cannot be uttered. Now He who searches the hearts knows what the mind of the Spirit is, because He makes intercession for the saints according to the will of God (Rom. 8:26, 27, NKJV).

CLOSING PRAYER . . .

Our Father, I pray that You would teach me to pray to You ever more effectively as I grow in my relationship with You. May my prayers take on real spiritual power, through the constant intercession of the Holy Spirit on my behalf. And may my prayers be pleasing to Your ears and directed toward the fulfillment of Your divine will in my life.

In Jesus' name, Amen.

HOW MUCH IS A CLOSE RELATIONSHIP WORTH?

Referring to faith and other things of God, all of us have our favorite stories that demonstrate how amazing the limitless powers of God can be and how we should invite God to use His powers to bless us through prayer.

A young man I knew was going through some very difficult times, financially. He lived in California, worked independently at home, and was having trouble both in getting work and in getting paid once he'd completed it. Eventually, he stood to lose his health insurance if he didn't mail a $600 payment, postmarked no later than the next day. However, he was scheduled to leave early in the morning to fly to an East Coast city and interview for a job.

That afternoon, at what he felt was the urging of the Lord, he called the head accountant of a company that owed him close to $5,000 and convinced the man to send him a check via FedEx, that very day, for overnight delivery. Then he visited his neighbor—a wonderful Christian himself who loved to witness to others—gave him a deposit slip, and made arrangements for the neighbor to intercept the check and deposit it immediately into the man's own bank account. Then he wrote his own check to the insurance company, stamped the envelope, and put it in his briefcase.

Late in the afternoon of the next day, from a city 2,000 miles away where his plane had landed for a layover, the man called his neighbor. "Did the check come?" "Yes it did!" said the neighbor. "And I took it to the bank, put it in your account, and talked about Jesus to three different tellers!"

At that point the man had a major decision to make. For some reason he felt that he desperately needed to keep his insurance. Yet he and his wife had always been blessed with excellent health, and he had plenty of other bills and commitments that were just as urgent. So he put the envelope containing the payment into a mailbox right there in the airport terminal, but he couldn't seem to let go and allow it to drop inside!

At that point he began to pray for God's guidance, with what seemed like half an airport full of people looking on. What should he do? Finally, he felt a sense of peace, thanked the Lord, opened his eyes, and let the envelope drop.

▼

▼

He didn't think about it again until 3 o'clock that morning when he woke up in his hotel room in the most intense pain he'd ever felt in his life. It soon became obvious that this was not something he'd eaten, and even if it were, he couldn't possibly deal with it on his own. So he looked in the yellow pages, found a hospital, grabbed his city map, and hobbled out to his rental car.

On the way to the hospital he couldn't sit still. He had to put his head out the window to keep from hyperventilating. When he finally got there, it seemed like hours before the emergency staff diagnosed his problem and gave him medication to reduce his agony.

Meanwhile, they had to call his wife to get permission to do the necessary surgery, since he was in no shape to agree to anything. Fortunately, he remembered the phone number of the teacher's clinic she was conducting half a world away, in Alaska!

Within a few hours they operated on him and removed a huge kidney stone. Later he went to his rescheduled appointment and did considerable work for the company (getting paid for it), even though he didn't get a permanent job.

A month or two later he saw the bill for all this. The whole episode cost almost $12,000, but since it had been an out-of-state emergency his insurance company had paid 100 percent.

God had worked out all the details in advance.

12

PROTECTING YOUR FAMILY

Thinking about how Satan invades a family brings to mind Job. His family paid a horrific price for what Satan was able to do while attempting to turn Job against God. Also, Joseph's brothers welcomed Satan into their midst and almost destroyed their family in the process.

> ### STRAIGHT FROM THE BOOK . . .
>
> *There's no such thing as a private, personal sin. Sin affects everybody close to the person who is sinning, including friends, fellow church members, neighbors, and coworkers.*

Job was a special case, however. Rather than concentrating on how Satan insinuates himself into our lives, the Book of Job shows how dedicated Job was to God.

Although the story of Joseph shows how Satan often works, it also shows a meaningful illustration of how God can turn anything around—even the vilest intrigues of Satan—to bring about His own good purposes.

ESTHER

Let's look at the story that has a villain who fully cooperated with Satan and attempted to destroy—not just a whole family—but an entire nation. The following selections from the Book of Esther illustrate the story of Esther and her cousin, Mordecai, who must have been somewhat older because he reared her as his daughter and counseled her accordingly. Esther's story is a *contrast* to the stories of Job and Joseph.

Mordecai and Esther were a family in what we might call the *small* or a *nuclear* sense. However, because they were both Jews, they were also part of a much *larger* family in God's eyes. That King Ahasuerus (known more commonly as Xerxes) did not know about Esther's heritage, when he selected her as one of his wives, makes what happened all the more fascinating.

The villain in the story is a man called Haman, about whom the Bible tells us very little except that the king elevated him to a very high position. Immediately, Haman got what we might now call the "Big Head" and demanded that everyone else bow to him and pay him special homage. For the same reason that Daniel refused to bow to King Nebuchadnezzar, Morcedai refused. Unfortunately, some other men reported (Esth. 3:4–6).

> Now it happened, when they spoke to him and he would not listen to them, that they told it to Haman, to see whether Mordecai's words would _____; for Mordecai had told them that he was a Jew. When Haman saw that Mordecai did not bow or pay him homage, Haman was filled with _____. But he disdained to lay hands on Mordecai alone, for they had told him of the people of Mordecai. Instead, Haman sought to _____ all the Jews who were throughout the whole kingdom of Ahasuerus—the people of Mordecai (NKJV).

(1) What was Haman's immediate response to Mordecai's "slight" of him?

_____

_____

(2) Yes or no—does his reaction seem a little extreme?

_____

(3) What do you know about how the world has often treated God's chosen people that might account for Haman's attitude toward them?

_____

_____

(4) What do you know about Satan that might explain why he pushed Haman so far, so fast? Satan can be sly, but is he known for a sense of restraint?

_____

_____

The story resumes in Esther 3:8–11.

Then Haman said to King Ahasuerus, "There is a certain people scattered and dispersed . . . in all the provinces of your kingdom; their laws are different from all other people's, and they do not keep the king's laws. Therefore it is not fitting for the king to let them _____. If it pleases the king, let a decree be written that they be _____, and I will pay ten thousand talents of silver into the hands of those who do the work, to bring it into the king's treasuries."

So the king took his signet ring from his hand and gave it to Haman . . . the enemy of the Jews. And the king said to Haman, "The money and the people are given to you, to do with them as seems good to you" (NKJV).

Please read the rest of the Book of Esther—it's a fascinating story. Many whole books have been written about Esther and the courage God gave her to match the challenge she faced. To summarize the main events, Esther risked her life to appear before the king, admit that she was a Jew, expose Haman's plot against her people, and ask the king to do what was right.

THE FEAST OF PURIM

For many years, orthodox Jews have celebrated the Feast of Purim. However, as with Hanukkah (the Feast of Dedication that Christ Himself observed in John 10:22), Purim is not one of the seven holy feasts that God ordained in the 23rd chapter of Leviticus. It's more of a social/religious holiday. At Purim, Jewish congregations often re-enact the events of the Book of Esther in colorful, often outlandish costumes and near-slapstick performances. The whole thing is often similar to old-time western melodramas—they even encourage the children to boo Haman and cheer for Esther and Mordecai!

Incidentally, the word "purim" is the plural form of "pur" (see Esth. 3:7), the ancient Hebrew word for "lot." Haman "cast lots" ("purim") to determine what day he would fulfill his diabolic plan to kill all the Jews in the kingdom.

Beginning with what Mordecai said to Esther when she reminded him of how dangerous it was for her to approach the king without permission and to ask for a favor, the passage says:

> And Mordecai told them to answer Esther: "Do not think in your heart that you will escape in the king's palace any more than all the other Jews. For if you remain completely silent at this time, relief and deliverance will arise for the Jews from another place, but you and your father's house will perish. Yet who knows whether you have come to the kingdom for such a time as this?" (Esth. 4:13, 14, NKJV)

Next we hear what could have been Esther's *final words*:

> Then Esther told them to reply to Mordecai: "Go, gather all the Jews who are present in Shushan, and fast for me; neither eat nor drink for three days, night or day. My maids and I will fast likewise. And so I will go to the king, which is against the law; and if I perish, I perish!" (Esth. 4:15, 16, NKJV)

Then, the tables begin to turn:

Then the king said to Haman, "Hurry, take the robe and the horse, as you have suggested, and do so for Mordecai the Jew who sits within the king's gate! Leave nothing undone of all that you have spoken."

So Haman took the robe and the horse, arrayed Mordecai and led him on horseback through the city square, and proclaimed before him, "Thus shall it be done to the man whom the king delights to honor!" (Esth. 6:10, 11, NKJV)

Finally, in chapter 7 . . .

Now Harbonah, one of the eunuchs, said to the king, "Look! The gallows, fifty cubits high, which Haman made for Mordecai, who spoke good on the king's behalf, is standing at the house of Haman."

Then the king said, "Hang him on it!" So they hanged Haman on the gallows that he had prepared for Mordecai. Then the king's wrath subsided (Esth. 7:9, 10, NKJV).

To answer some of the questions below, you might need to read a few more verses from Esther:

(1) How many Jews do you think lived in the land of Esther? Check one: ___ Dozens? ___ Hundreds? ___ Thousands? ___ Millions?

(2) Does the number really matter for this event?

_____
_____
_____
_____
_____

(3) Meanwhile, how many people were in agreement with Haman's trying to destroy all the Jews?

_____

_____

(4) How many people stood against Haman, for sure? Can you name them?

_____

_____

(5) The Bible does not tell us much about how Haman got his position as one of the king's most favored subjects, but given his character we can certainly speculate. Much more important, how did he fool the king into helping him put his evil, anti-Jew plan into effect? To what human emotions (which even kings have) did he appeal?

_____

_____

_____

(6) What qualities did Esther exhibit in her final answer to Mordecai and in what she did next?

_____

_____

(7) What would have been the penalty for her if she had failed?

_____

_____

(8) She did NOT fail, however. Why? Who was with her?

_____

_____

(9) What does this narrative tell us about the power of God versus the power of Satan?

_____

_____

STRAIGHT FROM THE BOOK . . .

At times the devil does not use a direct assault against a family's health or material possessions, but he will use an indirect tactic. He will tempt one member of the family to sin, and he usually begins with the father. If the devil can get a father to sin, he is well on his way to enslaving the entire family.

HOW SATAN INVADES A FAMILY

What does the discussion about Esther and Mordecai have to do with protecting your family? The connection might not be obvious at first, but think about it for a moment, and then answer the following groups of questions.

(1-A) Who was the most visible and vulnerable person in the story of Esther? (Hint: This person was the main focus of Haman's hatred.)

_____

_____

_____

(1-B) What was the corresponding family role this person fulfilled?

_____

_____

_____

_____

(1-C) Who is often the most visible and most vulnerable person in a family?

_____

_____

(2-A) Who had the most responsibility for guiding, counseling, and protecting the person who actually saved the Jews by interceding with the king?

_____

_____

(2-B) Who usually has primary responsibility for guiding, counseling, and protecting the younger members of a family?

_____

_____

(3-A) Against whom, in the Book of Esther, did Satan focus his attack?

_____

_____

(3-B) Against whom, in a family, does Satan often focus his attacks?

_____

_____

(4-A) In Esther 4:15, 16, what did Esther do to clarify and strengthen her resolve and to secure the blessing of God?

_____

_____

(4-B) What can you do to achieve the same result if you are a father or a mother?

_____

_____

(4-C) What can you do if you are a son or daughter?

_____

_____

(4-D) What can you do if you are a friend or a relative?

_____

_____

The following list of four items should be at the very top of *your* list, *especially if you are a father or a mother, rearing a family.*

(1) Recognize your position in Christ.
(2) Do what you know is godly.
(3) Be bold in your testimony about Jesus.
(4) Pray for your family.

Though *all* of these are important, which do you consider the *most* important, and why?

_____

_____

TELLING COMPARISONS . . .

The first column in the table below lists a number of biblical characters. The next column asks who stood with that person—God or Satan? The next columns ask who was against him or her (again, the choice is between God and Satan) and finally who won in the end. The last column asks you to identify the final result, in larger terms if you can. In other words, did what happened to that character affect anyone else? As you fill in the table you will see the pattern. Feel free to add any additional biblical characters you like to the first column.

Person	With Him or Her	Against Him or Her	Who Won?	Why? What Was the Final Result?
Abraham	God	Satan	God	His descendents became God's Chosen People
Nimrod				
Cain				
Jacob				
Joseph				
Balak				
Samson				
Ananias				
Jephthah				
David				
Judas				

THE STORY OF THE TALKING DONKEY

One of the most fascinating stories in the Bible is the story of Balak, Balaam, and Balaam's talking donkey! (For the donkey story only, see Numbers 22:21–29) Besides the talking donkey, this story is amazing because of the great number of lessons we can draw from it: (1) how God protects His people, (2) how often He does so, and (3) how foolish and futile it is to go against the will of God!

The story is told in the Book of Numbers—three relatively short chapters (22, 23, and 24). Read the entire text to see what happens when . . .

(1) A very foolish king (Balak) tries to hire a prophet (Balaam) to curse the Nation of Israel for . . .

(2) the purpose of rendering Israel powerless so that he (Balak) could defeat them easily.

(3) Balaam tries to comply and earn his fee, but he meets an angel sent from God, in a most convincing encounter. (The donkey finds his voice!)

(4) Three separate times Balaam warns Balak that he cannot defy God.

(5) Each time, Balak forces him to try anyway and gets the opposite result.

This story is another example of how God protects His own.

EZRA

The story of Ezra affords another glimpse of God's interest in families. Ezra led a small group of the Children of Israel out of the Babylonian captivity (48,000 of perhaps a million, or less than five percent), back to Jerusalem to rebuild the city, its walls, and the temple. What was the first thing he did when he and his band were a few miles down the road? (Ezra 8:21)

Then I proclaimed a fast there at the river of Ahava, that we might humble ourselves before our God, to seek from Him the right way for us and our little ones and all our possessions (NKJV).

Including this verse does not suggest that we *must* fast on a regular basis—although regular fasting by anyone who is physically able can be a wonderfully godly experience. Fasting, as practiced by both Ezra and Esther, is simply a way of intensifying the humbling of ourselves before the Lord, *in prayer*.

Equally important, note that Ezra said he was seeking help from God to know the right way "for us and our little ones." Regular prayer, not only for ourselves but for our families as well, is exceptionally important to God.

(1) Pray in the name of Jesus.

(2) Plead the blood of Jesus over your lives.

(3) Pray the Word of God.

(4) Pray with unwavering faith.

(5) Ask daily for the help of the Holy Spirit.

Absolutely nothing will help you stand against the snares, the fiery darts, and all the other wiles of the devil like regular prayer, on your knees (if you are physically able to do so) before God.

WORDS TO REMEMBER . . .

Or what man is there among you who, if his son asks for bread, will give him a stone? Or if he asks for a fish, will he give him a serpent? If you then, being evil, know how to give good gifts to your children, how much more will your Father who is in heaven give good things to those who ask Him! (Matt. 7:9–11, NKJV)

CLOSING PRAYER . . .

Our Father, give us a sense of urgency about protecting our families through prayer.

Help us to be faithful, every week, every day, and every hour. Even now we raise up the members of our families to You—for Your blessing, Your encouragement, and Your support. May all their relationships with You be strong and secure.

In Jesus' name, Amen.

STRAIGHT FROM THE BOOK . . .

To pray in the name of Jesus is not simply to say "in Jesus' name" at the end of a prayer. To pray in the name of Jesus is to pray what Jesus would pray on your behalf. It is to pray with an awareness of what God has promised to you, what is rightfully yours as a child of God, and what God has said He desires for you.

NOTES

---

1 From a video clip featuring Dr. Danny Ben-Gigi, former head of Hebrew Programs at Arizona State University and a renowned Hebrew scholar. Available at: http://www.israelnet.tv/program.html.

2 There is a downside to working with wet leather in warfare, of course. Centuries later, the American Plains Indians made their bowstrings out of buffalo sinews, which acted exactly like leather when they got wet. They stretched, and the bows became useless! Thus, these Native Americans learned to do their rain dances *after* their battles; never before.

3 I found the original list of definitions, on which I made minor adaptations, on the Web at http://www.whitestonejournal.com/seven/.

YOUR ENEMY IS STRONG.
THE BATTLE IS REAL.
PREPARE FOR VICTORY.

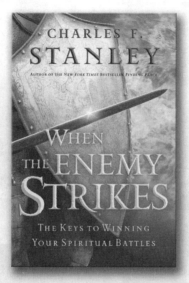

Fear, discouragement, loneliness, anger, temptation. These struggles are common to every human. Yet not all circumstances or negative emotions originate within. They could be the result of a willful, coordinated assault of Satan.

In *When the Enemy Strikes*, best-selling author Dr. Charles Stanley explores the often-overlooked reality of spiritual warfare—the tactics used by Satan to taunt, confuse, slander, and harm. Your adversary wants to crush your will, delay your promise, hinder your destiny, destroy your relationships, and lead you into sin. Dr. Stanley reveals how you should respond.

The battle is unavoidable, but take heart! God has given you the strength to stand.

NELSON BOOKS
A Division of Thomas Nelson Publishers
Since 1798

www.thomasnelson.com

DR. CHARLES F. STANLEY'S SERIES OF BIBLE STUDY GUIDES FEATURE insights and wisdom of this beloved pastor and author. Each title takes a unique fourfold approach to get the most out of Bible study time emphasizing personal identification with the Scripture passage, recognition of your emotional response, reflection of the passage's meaning and application, and taking steps to apply what's been learned.

Advancing Through Adversity (ISBN: 0-7852-7258-5)
Relying on the Holy Spirit (ISBN: 0-7852-7260-7)
Becoming Emotionally Whole (ISBN: 0-7852-7275-5)
Talking With God (ISBN: 0-7852-7276-3)
Listening to God (ISBN: 0-7852-7257-7)

ONLY
$7.99 EACH

NELSON IMPACT
A Division of Thomas Nelson Publishers
Since 1798

www.thomasnelson.com